The Empath Effect:

Powerful Stories of Love, Courage & Transformation

Alicia McBride

Are you an empath?

Find out here:

https://HealingLightEmpath.com/empathquiz

A great big thank you:

I would like to share a very special thank you with the following people. They have been kind, caring, and incredibly helpful to me on my journey through life. I wouldn't be where I am today without them. There are no words to properly express my gratitude. With all my heart, thank you!!

Alicia and Terry Phillips

Allyson Gelnett

Amanda Zook

Amy Largent

Christina Benz

Danielle White

Elaine Gelnett

Elyce Reynolds

Jess Regan

Julie Wesner

Kira and Todd Schaefer

Kristina Siefert

Mary Cameron

Michelle Burd

Misti Stroup

Nicole Bailey

Sabrina Watson

Shannon Griffin

Stephanie Snyder

Sylvia Barnhill

Tara Heisey

TC Reynolds

Ted Reynolds

I would also like to send sincere gratitude to every author in this book. Thank you for sharing your story, thank you for being vulnerable, and thank you for shining your beautiful light for the world to see.

Table of Contents

Foreword
By Alicia McBride

Imagine you meet someone new, and you instantly feel comfortable with them. You feel safe. You may share more with them in a few minutes than you have with others throughout your lifetime. You can't explain it, but they seem bright and open. Being near them feels natural. You are excited to share with them; you are happy to be around them. You can't believe how much came out of your mouth to a complete stranger in the grocery store.

That person is an empath. These are their stories.

These are stories about love, hope, death, courage, life, perseverance, recovery, transformation, and joy. These are real stories shared from the heart. You will probably laugh, cry, and feel a great deal of heart-swelling satisfaction. They are meant to inspire you and maybe change your life for the better. Each story is unique, but you can see we are all moving toward the same destination, with each author taking a different path.

The idea for this book was born out of my love of hearing other people's stories. I like being the empath in the grocery store with whom you overshare. You can share your troubles with me; I'm a safe space. I'm a deep feeler and a deep thinker. I don't care what you had for breakfast; I want to know what your life looks like, what makes you laugh, what makes you dance, and why you smile when it rains.

I gave these beautiful authors one task- tell me about your empath effect.

Empath Magic: A Beautiful Gift
By Alicia Mcbride

Empathic Author & Healer

It was three o'clock in the morning. The house was dark and quiet. I sat propped up on the couch feeding my newborn baby, staring at the phone, trying to stay awake. I searched for answers on the internet. Why did I feel this way? What was wrong with me? I was tired, and not just newborn-baby tired. My soul was tired, and it had been throughout my life. It felt like I had lived a thousand lifetimes.

Why did I feel so connected to everything yet somehow feel like an outsider? Why were there so few people in my life who truly understood me? Why was I always surrounded by arguing when all I wanted was peace? Was everyone right to say I was too sensitive? Did I need to toughen up and grow thicker skin? I felt everything, and I didn't like it.

Was it normal to feel everything? What was I?

I was definitely depressed, but this was more than that. This went beyond sad and tired. I felt like a wet sponge scrubbing a dirty floor. The floor was clean, but I felt yucky. There had to be something wrong with me.

Staying on the couch, with my now-sleeping baby lying on my chest, I contemplated these larger-than-life questions. I needed answers. I asked Google again and again. "Please Google, tell me what's wrong with me, so I can fix it," I said to myself. I liked fixing things, and I didn't want to feel this way anymore. "Just tell me what to do."

Then it happened. I saw the word "empath" and read the description. "Holy shit!" I thought to myself, how could one small word so perfectly explain my entire life?! I instantly felt relieved. There wasn't anything wrong with me! I didn't need fixing. I was sensitive, and being sensitive was okay. That night, in the middle of the night with a happily sleeping baby lying on me, I read everything I could possibly read about being an empath. I realized I had been taking on everyone else's energy and keeping it as my own. I did feel everything; I felt what was mine, what was others', and what belonged to the world. I realized I was drowning in feelings, and for the first time in my life, I was going to learn how to swim.

I took a deep breath and sighed in great relief. I felt better knowing there was an explanation for what I experienced, for realizing that I wasn't alone, and for recognizing there was nothing wrong with me. I put my phone down and kissed my newborn baby's head. Half smiling to myself, I realized I was going to find the peace for which I was searching. I closed my eyes for a few minutes.

Over the following days and months, I continued to read everything I could get my hands on. Books, articles, group chats, everything about empaths, spirituality, and soul healing. I also learned the words 'narcissist' and 'emotional abuse.' I learned about the narcissist/empath connection and how they seemed drawn to one another. This explained my marriage and why, despite five years of therapy, it was failing. As my eyes opened and I saw what was happening in my life, everything changed.

I lost some friends and gained some new ones. My "extra gifts" that were intermittently around throughout my life showed up in full force, all at once. I saw spirits of people and animals, deceased and living, had frequent psychic visions, and experienced other-worldly phenomena. I felt like Neo at the end of *The Matrix*, where Keanu Reeves holds out his hand to stop the bullets and says, "No." I felt like "The One." I didn't fear the change; I welcomed it and the difficult, wild ride that was ahead of me.

On Halloween afternoon in 2018, I was getting my kids ready for trick-or-treating at my mom's house. My best friend Amy texted me saying they were at urgent care with her daughter, Julia. She had a stiff neck and couldn't move it. In the early evening, she texted me again; they were in the hospital and found a tumor on her brain stem.

I stared at my phone in disbelief. My heart sank. My kids were having a great night trick-or-treating, and Julia was in the hospital with rare bone cancer. A week before, she was a normal one-year-old who happened to be really fussy. On Halloween, we found out why. I didn't know what to do, but I knew I needed to do something.

A few weeks later, on Julia's second birthday, I hosted a healing circle to send her healing energy. At the time, I had no idea what to do or how to do it. I kept receiving messages from "spirit" that gave me instructions, and I listened. I gathered a group of people in my home and online, and we held hands and crystals, and all sent her healing at the same time.

Almost two months later, Julia was given a week to live. I completely broke down. I fell to the floor on my knees, with my head buried in my hands, sobbing.

I drove to the hospital; I hadn't seen my best friend or Julia in months (I couldn't risk her getting a regular cold or flu during flu season), and I just needed to be there. During the drive, it was like my spirit energy reached out to Julia and said, "I'm on my way!" Our energy connected immediately, and I talked to her. It was crazy and amazing and unbelievable.

Weird ghost things happened to me throughout my life, and at this point, I knew about energy and healing, and I received messages from spirit, but this was advanced. It was different from anything I'd felt before - it was clear. I was connected to her, I could hear her, I could see her spirit, I could feel her. Up to this point, nothing as certain as this had happened to me.

Connecting with Julia's spirit in the car was amazing, and I'm grateful I was able to drive properly while talking to her. I arrived at the hospital, went into her room, and hopped right up in the bed. I had never sent healing like this before. I have sent my family and friends energy protections throughout my life, but this was different.

My body and soul knew exactly what to do. I felt it. It was like reaching down into this depth of being, understanding, and knowing. It was ancient and it was part of me. Thousands of people were already praying for Julia. I felt them all; the love, the prayers, the hope, and the sadness.

It was all-encompassing. This ancient healer came alive inside of me, and I channeled everything, right through my body and into her feet. It was incredible. I don't have the words to describe it properly. This little girl awoke something inside of me, and it couldn't be put away or ignored.

Julia put up a great fight against cancer. She held on long enough to be able to receive chemotherapy. She went through chemo and passed with flying colors; they even prepped the house for her coming home.

We have the most extraordinary capacity to feel, send, and receive love. Our depth of feeling has no limit; we feel with the greatest joy and the utmost sorrow.

During that time, my life continued to change radically. I was in the process of divorce, I finished writing my second book, my kids and I moved out, and I was far along on the spiritual path. I very clearly felt my calling.

On March 15th, 2020, Julia's body had enough. She passed away peacefully, and we mourned her loss deeply. I continue to learn, heal, and grow, and I give Julia the credit for where I am today. She helped me find my inner healer. I am grateful for her life.

Here's what I know about being an empath. We feel everything. We are sensitive. We are healers. We are magic. We are here to shine our lights brightly so we can heal ourselves and others. We have special gifts that allow us to connect to nature, to spirits, to animals, to humans, and to the universe.

We have the most extraordinary capacity to feel, send, and receive love. Our depth of feeling has no limit; we feel with the greatest joy and the utmost sorrow. We are here to help make the world a better place.

Being sensitive and feeling deeply is a powerful strength. It's a beautiful gift. What will you do with yours?

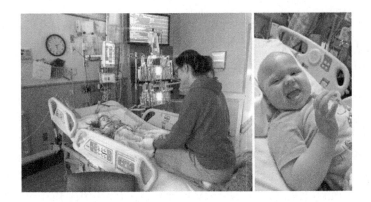

Alicia McBride is the internationally best-selling author of *I Feel Too Much: A How-to Guide for the Beginner Empath*. An empath and healer, she holds a B.A. in Psychology and is a reiki master and a certified yoga instructor. Alicia's calling is helping empaths and other highly sensitive people learn to let go of their excess energy, embrace their gifts, and accept themselves for who they are. Find her online at HealingLightEmpath.com; she would love to hear your story.

The Skeptic's Journey
By Willie Katinowsky

I think everyone has empathic abilities. Like all other aspects of existence, I believe some are born with a better connection to these abilities, but the potential is there for all to learn and develop these attributes. Whether unfortunate or not, I am predisposed to seamlessly experiencing the emotions of others. I am an empath.

Now, there are likely several definitions of what an empath is throughout this book, and they are all correct. But for the sake of clarity, I'd like to offer my own. For me, an empath is someone who experiences the emotions of others as if they are their own. Which, from my experience, can be incredibly confusing. It took me until I was about thirty to really grasp what was going on and develop a practice that helped me differentiate the feelings of others from my own.

From a young age, I was labeled as sensitive, though I am a July-born Cancer, so there is some validity to that label. But I also remember overhearing my parents tell a friend that I was emotionally explosive at times. Weirdly enough, this was never an issue in any setting other than at home, alone with my parents. I know many kids act out at home, but what I am referring to is outside the parameters of your average tantrum. I didn't understand it at the time, but I was experiencing my parents' emotions.

My parents are wonderful people and are liked by most who know them. With that being said, they were often verbally volatile towards one another behind closed doors during my childhood. I was told that we're not allowed to use excessively colorful language in our contributions to this book, so I won't be providing any quotes. I can say that my peers were in awe of the swear words and phrases that I knew and would often recite on the bus ride to Brecknock Elementary.

When these bouts happened, I was inundated with emotions that were out of the spectrum of what I could process as a child, mixtures of righteous anger, betrayal, and compunction. Not understanding that these feelings weren't mine, frustration and ultimately my own anger would then get worked into this unstable amalgamation of rage, and I would have a full-blown, Veruca-Salt-level episode.

Another common scenario that tested my empathic mettle was being around someone getting picked on. Kids can be cruel; we've all experienced this in one way or another. When I was around that as a child, I instantly froze because of the overwhelming assembly of emotions that I experienced.

My own curiosity and downright nosiness drew my attention to these situations, which I believe would open me up to the emotions of the event. It typically started with some general excitement at not knowing how this may unfold. A concoction of the bully's hate and authority would combine with the victim's grief and shame along with the myriad of emotions felt by the spectators. This would ultimately leave me virtually paralyzed in the moment and extremely exhausted afterward.

There were a few occasions when I would reflect on the event later in the day, usually at night, and would remotely tune into the victim's energy. Those memories are flagged in my brain because of the sheer intensity of the experience. As a practitioner of a few energy healing modalities, I now understand what I was doing in those moments. But as a child, I had no clue, and it could be emotionally devastating to process it all.

I don't mean to focus solely on childhood memories, but they tend to provide the strongest examples of my empathic episodes. As a result of these events' intensity, confusion, and frustration, I learned to subconsciously shut myself off as a defense mechanism. However, my adult life has not been entirely devoid of these experiences.

When I turned thirty, I made a myriad of helpful lifestyle changes as part of a commitment to become a more conscious being. This led to a spiritual awakening that dramatically altered the trajectory of my life.

One of the more fun experiences I've had as an empath took place shortly after my "awakening". I was living in southern California at the time and had just sat down to practice my guitar. I got a few chords into my warmup jam when, all of a sudden, I was hit by a wave of anxiety and a mental image of my friend Bixby (who happened to live in Pennsylvania, 3,000 miles away). The anxiety was specific to telling everyone about the baby that I was expecting. Now, I was single at the time and certainly had not recently sired any children. I was especially not anxious about telling anyone about this fictitious baby.

Quickly putting two and two together, I immediately reached out to Bixby and asked if his wife was pregnant. Sure enough, she was. Bixby was especially creeped out by my inquiry since they had not told anyone yet. In fact, they were planning to tell their families the following day at a gathering that they were hosting. What a coincidence, right?

Being a bit of a skeptic, Bixby still believes it was just a lucky guess, but it was obvious to me what had happened. If you are reading this because you too are an empath, then it's also likely obvious to you what happened.

We will always have to deal with something like this: the skepticism of others. This can be especially challenging when coming from those closest to us. But it's our responsibility to have faith in ourselves so that we can use these gifts to help others.

Energized by the implications of my experience with Bixby, I doubled down on my meditation practice and really started working on being aware of the emotions that I experience. I am certainly still susceptible to getting caught up in the feelings and emotions of others, but I have developed an incredible amount of control regarding how I respond to these emotions.

In order to learn to differentiate others' emotions from my own, I had to learn to observe all the emotions that I experience like they were separate from my own. This was an immensely difficult skill to learn and possibly even harder to maintain, but in this practice, I have learned that I am not my emotions. I am not anyone's emotions. I experience them, but I am not them. What this ended up giving me was the gift of freedom and the power of choice.

No matter the emotions' origins, I now have the power to choose whether or not I will act with the flow of what I am feeling. Of course, I slip up often, frequently in traffic, or when immensely frustrated. But all in all, this practice has allowed me to lean into my gifts rather than try to shut them down.

What this translates to is the power to help. When I'm chatting with a co-worker and feel their anxiety, I can ask some helpful questions and give them an opportunity to vent. In fact, this exact situation happened to me today (by today, I mean the day I'm writing this, as I have no idea what day you're reading this). When I pried a little, my colleague confided in me that he took his pregnant wife to the hospital last night due to a contraction scare. Everyone is great and healthy, and the pregnancy is still going as planned, but the situation was weighing on this person, and I could feel it.

I didn't know what, why, or any such details, but I knew there was something. As my friend was getting these feelings off his chest, I literally felt the anxiety/tension dissipate. This is the gift that we have to offer others: the ability to lighten their load.

This is the gift that we have to offer others: the ability to lighten their load.

I'd like to wrap up by adding a little bit of advice since I am confident that many who are drawn to this book are looking for other perspectives and ideas to further explore their own abilities. My advice is simple, and it's just to remember that there are no set rules to being an empath. Everyone experiences their gifts differently, and to complicate things further, this can change at any moment. I implore that you go easy on yourself, try not to judge (you or others) and most of all, use your gifts to navigate you into situations where you feel happy, fulfilled, and loved.

Sat Nam,

Willie

Willie Katinowsky is a father, an author, a musician, and a teacher of yoga and meditation. Outside of his current career in sales and marketing, Willie spends his free time encouraging others to embrace and explore the connection to their higher self. Coming from a more skeptical upbringing, he is committed to helping normalize the conversation surrounding the abnormal aspects of the spiritual journey. If you'd like to read more from Willie, you can check out his book *Spiritual as F*ck,* which is available on all major bookselling platforms. You can find him on Facebook at Spiritual AF Book or Instagram @spiritual_as_fuck_book.

The Poem
By Ashley Barnes

Poet, Author, Speaker, and Intuitive Leadership Coach

Fifteen years.

It was a hidden period of life when time stood still and kept moving all at once. A time when marriages started and dissolved, babies were born and grew, disparate families became one, and death became the demarcation of time.

One year since she died. Two years. Five years. Ten years. My mother, my best friend, gone. My creative voice, silent. Beautiful life transitions and what should have been joys underscored by great turmoil, pain, and unresolved grief.

All the while, something grew inside. Something that had always been there but had laid dormant since long before that day, fifteen years before, when the words of *The Poem* had been written.

Dormant because I had pushed it down, as we often tend to do. As a visionary, a natural healer, a tireless crusader for the human heart, I was too sensitive, too passionate, too loud – too much.

I learned to harness those qualities, to quiet my passionate voice, to not be a bother but rather be practically perfect. To fly below the radar just enough to stay connected but out of the way. To stay relevant but rarely noticed. To feel comfortable playing big only in my own imagination. And did I have an imagination! I channeled my passion into creative play and writing, mostly poems. Writing was my respite, my soul. It was who I was.

Until that day I didn't write anymore. The final poem, harvested from my old journal, held more truth fifteen years later than when it was originally written. Who knew the power it held to open magical, hidden doors to places inside I had only hoped existed?

Yet, when I opened my journal, I wasn't looking for transformation. I was simply reading. Curious. Hopeful. And so very tired. Ready to surrender, though I would hardly have admitted it. Then came the nameless poem. Then came that moment when the past meets the future, and nothing is ever the same in the present.

The moment I once again became a writer, a poet, a healer, an empath. *The Poem* was written on March 4, 1997, just eight days before my twenty-second birthday. I discovered it in a journal that had been packed away for years, with other memorabilia from my childhood.

The Poem:

It is moments

Like these when

I realize that I am

Empty.

You pour your

Soul out to

Me

And I watch you

Bleed, unfeeling

Unable to

Respond.

I am sorry, but

The only emotion I

Still feel is

Pain –

I feel it deeply and

THE EMPATH EFFECT

Often—

It overcomes nearly

Everything else.

It is old and

New and

Real.

I can no longer

Be close.

For too long,

I gave my love

Away,

Never to have it

Returned.

Love given,

Feeds on

Love received;

Otherwise it

Dies,

And mine has.

I want it back.

THE POEM

Reading *The Poem* for the first time in fifteen years, the sting of my own words on the paper bored through me like a thousand daggers piercing my flesh and finding their way straight to my heart. A lump formed in my throat as I read the words repeatedly. This poem was clearly a eulogy, a putting to rest of my life to that point, a very definite end. A death as real as putting me into the ground.

I may as well have been buried alive by my own words, for a part of me died that day. I don't remember the exact event that led to *The Poem*. It was written during a time of great turmoil. Pain. Unresolved grief. And silence.

My mother had terminal cancer. My parents were divorced. My beloved grandmother died. I was away at college with new friends, but I felt alone. Unloved. Disconnected. Whatever final straw happened to spark that anguish; it was clear to see where the pain became too much to bear. My final poem depicted my inability to feel, to give any more love to avoid the pain.

And so, I simply stopped writing, abandoning my last creative outlet – for fifteen years.

During that time of silence, I spent most of my life feeling out of control and drowning in stress, at the mercy and whim of everyone and everything around me. Like a leaf in the wind, floating around, blowing this way and that, always looking to others for guidance, shrinking from my natural gifts, never finding any respite from the influences around me.

I persevered by living life "by the book," for that's all I knew to do, despite never really feeling or thinking like anyone else around me. I felt alone. Unloved. Disconnected. The last line of *The Poem* clearly states my desires: "I want it back." All was not lost. The channel wasn't closed.

A new day

A new hope

Fears of the past

Still linger

Memories of where I've been

They made me

But they did not break me

They did not break me.

THE POEM

Little did I know that a chance writing class would inspire me to unearth my old journal. Little did I know that divine purpose was steering me back around to where I needed to be. Even after fifteen years.

As an "angel number," fifteen refers to new beginnings, a prompt to make much-needed changes, a harmony of matter and spirit. This poem was my new beginning. For in those moments when I found my journal and *The Poem* became real again, I became real again. For fifteen years, I had closed myself off. From my pain. From my joy. From my creativity. From my life.

Now the floodgates were open again. The feelings were accessible again. The walls were starting to come down. The healing could begin. The healing did begin. With it, the opening up of all that had been within me all along, just waiting to be rediscovered.

My deep sensitivity and passion, impeded as a child, came rising up to the surface, finally with a purpose that did not seem so overwhelming or shameful but instead endowed. The recognition, finally, that all those years of feeling out of place in nearly all jobs and social situations was because I really was different, in the best possible way.

The expansiveness of all this happening now, in this time and in this place, for my soul purpose of finally, finally putting me back together again. My journal couldn't end with *The Poem*.

After fifteen years, the first new poem I wrote went like this:

A new day

A new hope

Fears of the past

Still linger

Memories of where I've been

They made me

But they did not break me

They did not break me.

My experiences over the years made me. They prepared me. They wrapped me in a cocoon of pain, and when I crawled out of the chrysalis, I found myself a winged creator of my own hope, carrying hope for others.

I could finally stop hiding who I was and cultivate my best qualities – my natural sensitivity, compassion, intuition, and desire to do good for people – within any environment I found myself, despite the fact that it may not be embraced.

To simply be *me*.

With that, an enormous weight fell off. I still didn't fit in. I still cared about things others didn't. I still felt more than others around me. It was still hard in so many ways. But I was choosing a different path.

I wasn't hiding my empathic nature anymore. Instead, I was seeking out ways to use it, to incorporate it into my life instead of showing up as someone else each day. I was writing again, voraciously. Letting the words fall out, cleansing, and clearing the channels for more gifts to come in.

Most importantly to me, I was growing and using my gifts not only for myself but for the greater good. To be the change I wanted to see. As I believe I was always meant to do. As I believe most empaths are meant to do.

As empaths, we may feel like we've experienced more struggle and difficulty than others. We may have suffered at the hands of others due to our sensitive natures and compassionate hearts. We may feel like we never fit in anywhere. Those deep wounds deserve our love, attention, and healing.

Yet, we are also the visionaries. The wounded healers. The tireless crusaders for the human heart. As such, we are uniquely positioned to be a catalyst for change. To help birth a new paradigm of being for all people, most especially for ourselves. When we heal, others heal. When we open to our gifts, we give others permission to do so as well. When we touch our finger to the cosmic pool, it ripples out and touches everyone.

As empaths, this is our birthright. This is our purpose. We have the opportunity to create the future we want to see, not by becoming something new but by tapping into who we came here to be.

My challenge for each of us is to awaken to the wounds that keep our much-needed voices silent. To keep doing our healing work, even though it may be painful and difficult. Because, in doing so, we ensure that our experiences don't break us but instead allow us to keep inspiring change and revealing to ourselves, and everyone else, what we already are – the light the world needs.

THE POEM

We can no longer ignore, in fear and distrust,

What we know in our bones to be true,

For it is in us, it IS us

And we are a light for the world

From The Rising: "A Light for the World"

Ashley Barnes is a poet, author, speaker, and intuitive leadership coach. After a lifetime of trying to diminish her own deep sensitivity, and nearly giving up on her authentic self in the process, Ashley has learned how to flourish while also honoring her natural gifts.

Drawing from the wisdom and insights gained through her career in corporate leadership development and her own healing journey, Ashley guides visionaries, change-makers, and spirit-led women to develop their inner knowing and create a life full of joy, ease, and lasting impact! To learn more, visit Ashley at http://www.ashleybarnes.guide.

Energetic Strength
By Jen Schmitt, MCLC, RMT

Energy is my first language. I know it better than the English I speak. I feel things differently and on a deeper level than the average person. My body feels energetic exchanges and subtleties to humans, animals, places, and things. I pick up on everything, and I can tell someone exactly what they're feeling. It resonates inside of my body, and I can read a person before they can open their mouth to speak. I have a magnetic and intuitive connection with animals. They approach me as if they know I understand them. We have an energetic dialogue, and I know what they're saying and feeling.

There are places I've been where I've experienced physical and emotional reactions towards the events that took place there, and even the people present during said events. I can feel storms coming, even in the middle of the night while sleeping. I can sense the pressure change and energy from them, and I wake up seemingly for no apparent reason and lay there, unable to go back to sleep. Like clockwork, within 10-15 minutes, I'll hear a distant rumble of thunder. I have a remarkably heightened awareness of energy changes around me and within my own body. I'm a giant energy magnet, human barometer, lightning rod, antenna, bioenergetic, and I'm an empath.

I have always been the go-to person for family and friends needing a shoulder or some advice. Complete strangers come up to me and share their life stories, tales of woe, and frustrations. People share their problems, and every emotion, feeling, and vibration they've been holding on to is cast out of them.

Being the emotional sponge that I am, I absorb it all, allowing them to feel better after, but I am left feeling like shit. For the longest time, I thought it was because I was naturally empathetic to their needs, stories, feelings, etc. Even though I am empathetic, the actual emotions and feelings I was experiencing weren't entirely mine. They belonged to someone else, and I was receiving them blindly and mistaking them for my own. There was never any warning, explanation, or permission, which made it incredibly difficult for me to decipher to whom the emotions truly belonged. I felt like an antenna tuned in to all of the frequencies, all of the time.

As an empath, this is common. We would give someone the shirt right off our backs, our last dollar, and even our right arm if we knew it would make them feel better. When someone is in need, we're first on scene, always there to help. We're service-oriented people, and it's our nature to want to help, fix, please, and be everything to everyone. We're notorious for spreading ourselves thin, people-pleasing, and not knowing how to say "no."

Giving so much of ourselves is exhausting for an empath. We have big hearts and big feelings; it's who we are. I'm often accused of being "too sensitive," "fragile," "over-emotional," "dramatic," and "too much." I've been told to "suck it up," "it's not that bad," "you think too much," and "you need thicker skin" more times than I can count, and my personal favorite, "The world is going to chew you up and spit you out if you can't get a grip on reality."

Reality. I love this word. Ok, I'm oozing sarcasm here. I'm dramatic, though! To a lot of people, it seems like I'm off my rocker.

I don't fit the mold of their reality, and they have zero clue about what life is like as an empath.

However, these supercharged feels I experience every single day of my life are quite my reality. I don't know what it's like to not feel everything all of the time. They call it crazy; I call it a typical Tuesday. These words hurt and left me feeling like I was weird, out of place, damaged, and cursed. I wanted to scream. I felt lost and alone, and no one seemed to understand me or my experiences.

Empaths have a highly tuned nervous system, and it's extremely easy for empaths to become overwhelmed since our emotional buckets fill so quickly. We tend to have this underlying belief that we're hard to love because we're so deep and severely misunderstood. We long to feel that someone understands us, and we're confused as to why people don't "get" us because we "get" everyone.

For this reason, we tend to seek out love in all the wrong places. It's not uncommon for an empath to be swept off of their feet by a narcissist. The empath/narcissist relationship is one of extremes, good and bad. They're like a moth to each other's flame, and this fatal attraction is incredibly unhealthy and destructive. The narcissist loves the attention they receive from the empath because they're so caring and nurturing.

The empath is all too eager to give, and give, and give. All of their time, support, energy, whatever they need, no expense is spared, which is exactly what the narcissist wants. The empath loves the attentiveness and seemingly understanding from the narcissist. They make the empath feel like they're the most amazing thing on Earth to happen to them, and they understand their depths. I later learned the term "love bombing" because this is how the relationship starts, and the empath, seeking to be loved and understood, falls, hook, line, and sinker.

My first marriage was this exact relationship. He was the way cool, slightly older guy who was a thrill-seeker, funny, smart, outgoing, and fun. He seemed nurturing, and he understood me. He was extremely doting and protective, and I shared very vulnerable things about myself as he made me feel safe and that I could trust him. Slowly, the doting turned into neglect, everything raw about me that I shared with him, all of my quirks and my triggers were flipped on their heads and used against me to manipulate me for his control.

The protectiveness turned into possessiveness. It was an emotionally and mentally volatile relationship. Everything was about him, his needs, his wants, his desires, and his happiness. His problems were my problems, and my problems were my problems. Eventually, the mental and verbal abuse turned physical. His anger and rage I absorbed, and the energy behind it I took on was deep cutting pain, sorrow, abandonment, and tons of insecurities.

I felt sorry for him, so I blamed myself for triggering him. He would "apologize" but then blame me for triggering him. I felt that he was struggling in a dark place, and I wanted to help. It was my personal assignment to "fix" him, and I exhausted so much of my energy trying to do just that. I couldn't even see what was actually happening because I was in such denial. I didn't want to believe this man who I loved, and who was so good to me initially, was this horrible and selfish person that hurt me in the deepest of ways, intentionally, for his own gain and satisfaction.

Marriage is about give and take, and that's exactly what happened. I gave and he took, and took, and took until I was gassed with nothing left to give. It's difficult for others to understand the courage and strength it takes to leave these situations. It's easy to say, "Just get out!" but when you're designed to fix, heal, and support, it's not that simple. I finally found the courage and strength I needed to leave, only to get swept up over and over in different but more of the same relationships.

Relationships are incredibly difficult for me. I've been divorced three times. I don't trust easily, as you can imagine. My insecurities only grew after each failed marriage. I had my guard up in all the wrong places and very little self-respect and self-love to set healthy boundaries. I always felt that I was never good enough but too much at the same time.

I felt like no one understood me, loved me, or even wanted to. I was the only one picking up the pieces, and I learned to rebuild myself time after time, but there were beautiful pieces of me omitted with every blow. I learned a lot about what I didn't want in marriage, but I didn't know what I wanted or needed because I lived my life trying to please everyone else. I was my own afterthought and everyone else's.

My triggers are plenty. It's no wonder empaths tend to suffer from depression and anxiety. I've suffered from anxiety for the majority of my life. I have been off and on various medications over the years and, through trial and error, learned these medications and I don't jive. I experience horrible side effects from them. I had major headaches, I couldn't focus, the ADHD was in overdrive, I couldn't sleep, I was nervous, had muscle spasms and tremors, and I gained 40 pounds in one year.

At some point, by the grace of God, I started to become aware that I had no feelings. I wouldn't cry over a tragic event such as a death, which is something I would normally have fallen to pieces over. Not one tear. I was completely numb. I felt nothing and didn't care about anything. It seemed like all of my emotions had left me. I started researching the medication I was on and learned one of the biggest side effects was suicidal thoughts. I could see why.

I needed off of this medication, but the doctor wasn't exactly on board. So, I took matters into my own hands and slowly weaned myself off over the course of 6-8 weeks. The withdrawal effects from this medication were even more horrendous than the side effects from taking it. They've been compared to that of a heroin withdrawal.

I had night terrors, random twitching and spasms all day, and in my sleep, my eyeballs bounced side-to-side every time I turned my head. The zaps. The zaps were especially fun. They're called the zaps because they would hit without warning and would feel like my brain was being electrocuted. It took an entire year for these withdrawal symptoms to fully stop, my head to clear, my emotions to return, and the weight I had gained to start falling off.

I vowed to never take this shit again. In 2015, I was going through a rather difficult journey with post-partum anxiety. It was at this time I found reiki. Through my reiki healing sessions and meditation, I discovered that I'm a healer. I'm now a reiki master teacher, thanks to my anxiety struggles and being an empath.

I didn't know what an empath was until I was in my mid to late 30s. When I heard the term and what traits and common experiences are for an empath, I knew instantly that the shoe fit. This discovery finally allowed me to answer a lifelong question but with it came even more questions. There was more to it, and I knew it because there's more to me. I have these empath traits and then some. I feel energy in a way that isn't typical; in fact, I sense things in multiple ways. I already knew I was an intuitive and clairvoyant, but there was more to discover. Down the rabbit hole I went, and I learned about the different types of empaths. I'm an intuitive empath.

I visited Oklahoma City in the spring of 2019 and took the opportunity to tour the memorial on the site of the 1995 bombing. I was in high school when this happened, and I vividly remember the news coverage of the event and the horror that transpired. However, nothing could prepare me for the experience of visiting ground zero. I had never been to Oklahoma City before, and as we drove through the streets of downtown, I knew when we were close to the site.

We were approximately a block away when my chest tightened up, and every hair on my body stood on end. The moment we rounded the corner toward the entrance, I felt a massive shock wave go through my entire body. I actually felt the percussion of the blast. By the time we pulled up in front of the memorial, I could barely breathe. It felt like a thousand elephants sitting on my chest.

The sights alone are enough to take in, with an incredibly beautiful tribute constructed from such a heinous tragedy. It's also extremely heart-wrenching. It's impossible for me to imagine anyone wouldn't be moved by being there, but what I was experiencing wasn't typical. I could hear the screams, the sirens, I felt the fear, terror, and utter confusion. Hell, I could see it. The feeling of intense pain and indescribable sadness took root inside of my body.

You're so much more than you've been led to believe, and if you embrace this strength in you, doors of abundance will open.

I cried and fought tears throughout much of the tour. It was a completely surreal experience standing there 24 years later and feeling the energy of the entire place engulf me. It was suffocating, and it was a lot. I've been many places, and I've had tons of these experiences in the past, but this was by far the heaviest I've ever felt.

For me, being an empath has had its challenges. There have been plenty of times where I hated feeling so much. It's not easy. I wanted to escape, crawl in a hole, and stay hidden forever. Having all of the "feels" all of the time can become unbearable. Eventually, I learned how to protect my energy with healthy coping mechanisms through various means of holistic therapies and practices, and I've learned proper self-care, self-love, and boundary setting.

Through all of this, I've grown to love being an empath! It's a beautiful gift to be able to feel so deeply! I learned how to make this and all of my other amazing and powerful gifts work for me. I'm a lightworker, intuitive empath, clairvoyant, and clairsentient. Now, psychic mediumship is tapping me on the shoulder. These parts of me serve me rather well.

I'm able to help, serve, and heal the world in a way not just anyone can. Everything I've been through has paved the way for this road I'm on. I'm fulfilling my life's purpose as a reiki master teacher and intuitive spiritual life coach because of my life's experiences as an empath. I will continue to walk this path as I help others discover their gifts and magic, help them heal, embrace, and cultivate their gifts to work for them, just as I have done.

To some, I may seem too sensitive, fragile, or over-emotional, but I'm so much stronger than they realize. They may say I'm dramatic or too much; those aren't my people, and they should go find less. Some may think I need thicker skin, but I like my permeable, thin skin because it allows me to feel love, compassion, and empathy on a deeper level. Maybe I do think too much and make things ten times harder than they should be, but I always find my way, in my own way.

While it seems I've been "chewed up and spat out" a few times, I've always found the strength and courage to persevere. The world sure as hell hasn't swallowed me whole, and I'm not about to let it. People can only understand from their level of perception. Given that empaths make up a small fraction of the people here on Earth, we're a part of a very unique, exclusive club with special, indispensable gifts. You're so much more than you've been led to believe, and if you embrace this strength in you, doors of abundance will open.

Jen Schmitt, MCLC, RMT, is an intuitive spiritual life coach and reiki master teacher who is dedicated to helping highly sensitives and empaths embrace and nurture their gifts so they may light their souls on fire and live their best lives. You can find her at JenSchmittCoaching.com.

Room for the Light
By Alli Blair Snyder

They tell you that your life can change in a moment; one fraction of a breath, and the very trajectory of your existence can be irrevocably altered.

I mean, I have heard people say that before, but I always thought the horrific stuff happened to "other people." My new husband and I - we had just become "other people." The grief that followed the moment I fully understood that our baby was gone hit me like a freight train to the temple. It felt as if I was wading through a deep and terrifying jungle, where I had previously only walked the perimeter. Now I was plunged headfirst into the darkness of it, naked and barefoot, with no light to find my way out.

No amount of loss or growth I had ever experienced before could have prepared me for this; no map I held could give me steps to follow. I had no idea who I was anymore. I felt lost and alone, and all hope I had for my future, our future as a family, was extinguished. I stopped breathing. I became shattered glass, whose fractured edges cut anyone who got close to me, even people I loved the most. I stayed broken and in the caves of that dark and musty jungle for a very long time.

On the surface, I strung myself together as best as I could in order to shower and get to work and put food in my dog's bowl and ask my husband how his day was. You know, the normal, everyday stuff that still needs done even when it feels like the world has ended. Maddeningly, the sun kept rising in the morning and setting at night. I decided that I needed to find a way to move myself if I was still going to be here. "Here," as in earth. Alive. I asked myself that a few times, actually. "Alli, do you still even want to be here now that Finn is gone?" Most of the time, in the beginning, the answer was a deafening "no." I didn't. I felt the pain every moment I breathed.

I knew there was a difference between surviving and living; all I had done up to that point in my grief was simply keep my head above water. I decided I needed to rip and tear the hastily formed scabs over my wounds to work fully through the pain. I needed to bleed out, figuratively; I had to come face to face with my demons. I needed to come to understand the difference between sorrow and grief. I needed to find a way to breathe again, to have hope, to find love for myself. I needed to build a new normal. So, I started paying attention to everything I was feeling.

Here's the thing with letting a dam loose - all of the water, even the dark and murky stuff way down at the bottom, comes rushing out. The darkest stuff comes out last. When you think everything's already drained, the worst of it comes trickling out at the end. The truth is that losing our son, Finn, was the breaking point and the catalyst for shattering that wall. I had dark secrets buried deep inside that hadn't seen the light of day in years, feelings and emotions I had long since shoved down or drowned with alcohol.

I had been through so much leading up to my son's death that I never spent the time working through it all. Finn was my third child; before him, I had two painful and heart-wrenching abortions. I sometimes vaguely say I miscarried them to avoid saying it; sometimes, I neglect to mention those two little babies at all. The shame, the guilt, was more than enough to drown me. Since losing Finn, I have miscarried our fourth baby. One of my darkest thoughts is feeling like my body is a graveyard.

I'm writing this from inside the cave today, the one in which I have become so familiar. Everything feels dark and murky, but I've been down here long enough to let my eyes adjust. I know every crevice and texture of the walls, the earth beneath me, the blackness around me. The shadows move in and out of my vision, new ones this time and ones I know intimately. Light flickers every once in a while, and I catch it on my face. The warmth of that glow is the hope that I need. I know soon I will have the strength to stand and begin to walk out into the jungle and into the sunshine beyond. But after many, many times down here, I know this to be true - this process, it takes work.

This cave is where I went inside my mind after each moment of trauma I experienced in my life. I didn't always understand what it was, or why I was there, or what it meant. But if I'm going to explain to you my story of being an empath, someone who has the capacity to feel all the things and recognize those feelings in other people, I have to start here. In the cave of my mind, soul, and feelings.

Here is where I learned what it means to feel things deeply, down in my bones, at the very core of my being. Here is where I understood that it's okay, valid, and important to feel. It's here that I became comfortable feeling the dark things, the light things, the heavy things, and the joyful things, and everything in between. All of the facets of our human capability of experiencing life. I've come to know this as a gift. I didn't always see it that way.

The first time I became conscious of this cave and how I created it in my mind was after I tried to die. Finn had died a few weeks prior. Five feet from me, five days before Christmas, he breathed for five minutes - and then he stopped. I didn't know or understand how to keep breathing and living after he was gone.

The pain hit me like a Mack truck to the temple. The drowning sadness, the seeing-red rage, the out-of-my-skin anxiety, the catching-my-breath PTSD visions of his death, and the expectation to handle all of this and go back to work. It's not entirely that I wanted to die and leave everyone I loved - it's that I didn't know how to live in this new, unfathomable reality. I remember thinking as I swallowed the pills and chugged down the wine that I hoped I didn't wake up. What I really meant was that I hoped I would wake up from the nightmare my life had become.

Alcohol was a delicious means to numb the feelings I had for most of my life. I can't remember a time when I didn't feel everything to a degree that felt impossible to handle, even before Finn died, so I found many ways over the years to numb it or shove it down. I did anything to avoid feeling. When I was made fun of and pushed into lockers in middle school, I threw myself into soccer practice. When I was sexually assaulted in high school, I smoked as much weed as I could get my hands on. When I sustained multiple brain injuries through car accidents and sports games and subsequently was pulled from my college soccer team after my fifth concussion on record, I had sex with boys.

After every breakup, every failed college class, every fight with my parents because my brain felt out of my own control and they just couldn't understand my behavior, after every baby I lost - I drank. A lot. Alcohol became my numbing drug of choice and my closest confidant and friend. Alcohol made the cave I was plunged into time and time again feel not so alone and not so dark. It softened the edges and blurred the shadows.

I wish with almost every fiber of my being that I could drink right now. To numb the shadows and blur the edges. Everything feels sharp and raw. Sometimes I stand in the aisles where they sell wine and beer in the grocery store and get some weird looks. My belly protrudes so far out that I can't even see my shoes, so it makes sense. Eight months pregnant and salivating over the selection of Francis Coppola isn't easily understood by just any passerby. In my fifth pregnancy in nearly eight years, and the cave is more familiar to me than ever. And goddess, that wine would taste just so good right now.

I'm in the middle of feeling it all, sitting in the depths of the darkness, both intimately familiar and new all the same. Two abortions, a late-term loss, and a miscarriage all led to trying for almost a year to conceive this tiny little being beating his heart just below mine. I want the wine, or anything to numb this a little bit, because I'm being forced to feel everything.

Everything. The trauma, the pain, the grief, resurfacing with every ultrasound and doctor's appointment. The PTSD and anxiety creeping in. I begrudgingly walked myself into my cave, raw and alone. But this is the only way. This is what I teach people; this is what I've practiced. I'm calling on myself to remember how I began to see this ability I have as a gift.

In the years after I woke up from trying to die, I went on a journey of figuring out how to be in that cave. I ended up being able to see other people more clearly, the more I sat with myself. I realized that the depth of darkness I now knew and understood gave me the ability to see that depth in other people. To hold space for their darkness, their edges, their shadows. I am more able to help them walk around and navigate their own caves. But it took me doing the work of embodying those feelings myself.

I found that the more I numbed or drank away my feelings and emotions, the nastier and more intense they became. I wasn't necessarily making them go away; I was simply putting duct tape over their mouths and ignoring them lurking at me from the corners of my brain. When the alcohol wore off, they were pissed.

At first, they attacked me with a vengeance, stronger than before, ripping the duct tape off and coming in so big I couldn't ignore them. It looked like spontaneous hysterics on the phone with my mom. Screaming at my husband for something ridiculous. Sobbing tears in my car before walking into the office. Spending all of my paycheck at Target as soon as it hit my bank account. Running fifteen miles, to the point of exhaustion, and nearly collapsing on the side of the road. And so, I'd go back to drinking because it seemed more stable than all of this. Rinse, repeat.

It wasn't one specific breaking point when I understood this could no longer be my life but a series of small realizations. One, in particular, stands out in my mind. At one point during one of my cycles I just described, I realized I hadn't smiled in about a week. Not once. At anyone. And it must have become somewhat of a new normal for me because no one even mentioned it. This was a few months after Finn died, and I woke up.

It hit me that when I was working so hard to not feel the dark and hard things, I was effectively preventing myself from feeling anything else as well. Happiness, joy, relief, contentment, pleasure, curiosity, hope. I couldn't remember how to call those up or allow them in. So, I did something that, to this day, I teach people how to do. I spent time with the only emotions that were showing up - my demons, as I used to call them.

I went into my cave. I pulled out a notebook, and I called each of them by name: Rage, Sadness, Grief, Shame, Fear. In my mind, I sat in front of each of them, and I saw no way around them. They were unmoving, looking at me. I said the only thing I could think of, "What do you need?"

They told me. My Rage needed to move me. My Sadness needed to be released. My Grief needed space to breathe. My Shame needed to be healed, softly. My Fear needed to be acknowledged and understood.

*No matter how dark things become,
there is always room for the light.*

As I took the time to give each of them what they needed, I felt my demeanor shifting. I laughed with my husband for the first time either of us could even remember, and I knew. I knew feeling the hard things paved the way for this. It opened up the space. It allowed the light to peek through the shadows.

Sitting in the cave now, in the middle of the hardest season of my life, I do remember why this practice is a gift. My entire pregnancy has been incredibly trying; surgeries, medications, hospital trips. All in an attempt to allow this baby to live in a place where all of our others have died. It's brought up every single feeling from the past. Sometimes I do think about my old friend, a glass of deep red wine, to take some of the pain away. To numb and soften my sharp edges. But this space of feeling everything is truly a gift.

Allowing myself to get comfortable down here in the darkness, allowing myself to feel all the difficult feelings - it's created the space to feel hope that this time things will finally be different. I've taught people how to navigate feeling everything to the nth degree, how to allow their eyes to adjust to the darkness, how to welcome their feelings and emotions and call them by their names, how to ask them to become their teachers - all from the earthy floor of my own cave while I do the same.

They tell you that your life can change in a moment. One fraction of a breath, and everything becomes different. For me, it broke the ground beneath me and dropped me into the cave. From here, I emerged understanding myself as an empath, with an ability to understand the people around me and the compassion to recognize their darkness. Living a life as an empath has many incredible facets and gifts, and I hope in reading this book you feel part of a beautiful community of humans. I hope you feel not so alone in your ability to feel... everything. Deeply. Fully. Truly.

This is the facet I feel most strongly about. When we allow our feelings to speak to us and tell us what we need, they transform from being something we avoid - our demons - to something we can learn from. Our teachers. The darkest nights we walk through allow us to appreciate and welcome the brightest sunshine days. The depths of shadows we have known in ourselves allow us to recognize and hold space for the depths of shadows in other people. It reminds us that no matter how dark things become, there is always room for the light.

Alli Blair Snyder is a storyteller. When she isn't writing or buried in a book, she is snuggled up with her rescue dogs, husband, and new baby Rowan in their little Pennsylvania town. She is a writing professor at Alvernia University and Ph.D. candidate in Leadership Theory, focusing on shame and resilience. She is also a medicine woman, Celtic reiki master, trauma-informed mental health coach, and master shadow work healer who fiercely advocates for becoming the expert of your own life and healing. Connect with her via alliblairsnyder.com.

THE EMPATH EFFECT

Becoming Real
By Alyce Martin

You become. It takes a long time. That's why it doesn't often happen to people who break easily, or have sharp edges, or who have to be carefully kept. Generally, by the time you are Real, most of your hair has been loved off, and your eyes drop out, and you get loose in the joints and very shabby. But these things don't matter at all, because once you are Real you can't be ugly, except to people who don't understand. From The Velveteen Rabbit by Margery Williams

It was only two years ago that I think I actually fully and completely inhabited my body. I was sitting in my office at work talking to a coworker, and I thought to myself, "I'm really here." It's hard to explain, but it was almost as if I finally felt real. It was terrifying and exhilarating on the surface layer, but at my core, it felt like I was finally "home." You see, most of my life, I was not fully in my body. I understand now that a big part of it was unresolved trauma, but another piece of the puzzle is that I am an empath. In other words, I feel all the feels. Some say this is a heavy cross to bear. I agree, and yet, I wouldn't change who I am or what I've experienced even if I could.

I was always a "sensitive kid." I remember receiving that message often when growing up, usually in reaction to my expression of what felt quite deep and intense at the time. "You're being too sensitive" or "You're okay" were said to me often by family, teachers, adults - the people who I assumed knew more about life than me.

I internalized this idea that "I was too sensitive" and that this was a serious problem. The worst part was I didn't feel "okay." I felt intense emotions as a kiddo and didn't know how or have the resources to learn how to process my experience. I began to feel unsafe expressing my feelings the way I knew how so I did what most people do: push them down and bury them deep inside. Eventually, the pressure would build, and they would release in an explosion. But some of them got stuck inside, cloaked in shame. Those feelings I learned to keep at bay, afraid to let anyone see. After all, they were my defects. I must have done something wrong. *I* was wrong.

In truth, I was having a human experience, and a part of my personal human experience is that I identify as both a highly sensitive person and an empath. As such, I am hyper-aware and tuned in to the energy of my surroundings and have a strong propensity to absorb that energy. As a child, I didn't know how to discern others' frequencies and emotions from my own. Certainly, being around vibrations that felt uplifting was lovely, but, on the flip side, encountering energies that felt heavy and dark was especially uncomfortable because I felt them so intensely.

I came into the world with this sensitivity, and as such, I didn't have the language to explain what I was experiencing to the adults in my life. Attempts made to do so were dismissed or met with discomfort in the beholder. This was no one's fault. It was just what happened. At any rate, I learned to leave my body in order to feel safe. As a result, most of my childhood is a blur, with small patches of memories. Things get clearer in the teenage years but are still fuzzy. Even in my 20s, I didn't spend much time present in my human form.

I always felt different, like there was something wrong with me. Like I was an alien on this planet.

I was quite honestly shocked by all of the horrific wrongdoings and the pain and the suffering and injustice that I saw and *felt* all around me. Yes, I felt love and joy, also, but I couldn't shake the other stuff. I was sure the world was falling apart, and I had made a serious mistake in coming here. Or perhaps, I must have done something terribly wrong to be surrounded by and feel all this pain. I would ask myself, "How could this stuff happen?" and "How is everybody alright with this?" Some days I still do.

As a way to feel like I was doing something to shift the energies I didn't like feeling, I learned to play the role of the caretaker. It made me feel better to make sure that people in my life were happy and content. I might not have been able to process my emotions, but I had an innate ability to listen to others and help them work through their stuff. I learned I liked helping. I had wisdom about life, a deep knowing about things that I believe come from past lives. Yet, I couldn't understand why life had to be full of so much suffering.

Middle school, like many preteens, was an especially turbulent time in my life. I was bullied for being different, which only fueled the core belief that something was wrong with me. Amongst the tough times, there were very bright spots. When I was twelve, I was gifted with the opportunity to attend a summer camp. Away from my life at school, I was a different person. I made some sweet friends and felt accepted. I got into theater and dance, which were amazing outlets for me. Performing was a way I could express myself that felt relatively safe.

As I moved into my middle teenage years, I experienced periods of depression coupled with significant fatigue and digestive issues. Medication and therapy helped marginally, but I couldn't shake feeling unwell in my physical body. I began to believe this was normal. In my late teenage years, I began using relationships, sex, food, and exercise as means of numbing myself while at the same time trying to feel something other than pervasive pain and discomfort. Perfectionism was always a means of feeling safe, but it became my drug in my early 20s. I controlled my diet meticulously and exercised my body to the point of exhaustion. I lost my menstrual cycle for almost a year and developed hypothyroidism.

Luckily, my angels, the universe, God, something greater than me, is always conspiring to help me see the light, placing nuggets of wisdom and sweetness along my journey. After graduating from college, I was blessed to move to the majestic Rocky Mountains of central Colorado. Their peaceful, grounded energy helped save me from myself. I connected with open-minded people and spent a lot of time in nature. I had learned a form of energy healing called reiki a few years prior and began to connect with people who shared this calling and started to see its power in my own life.

I continued to search for understanding of my experience, and my soul yearned for deeper healing. I studied alternative healing methods, including naturopathy, energy medicine, nutrition, meditation, and yoga. Along the way, I kept hearing the term "empath" and later "highly sensitive." As I learned more about both, I felt seen and validated. I felt less alone. There were others out there like me! The puzzle pieces began to fit together.

My life began to make sense: the toxic personal and even professional relationship dynamics I continually seemed to attract, the periods of dissociation, the short bouts of depression and anxiety inconsistent with any particular mood disorder, the way I could be moved to tears by only a few notes of music. It was like my story was unfolding before my eyes in a way I hadn't been able to see before.

This understanding helped me to know there wasn't something wrong with me, just something different. Having this knowledge allowed me to move forward in my spiritual development by leaps and bounds. All that I learned during my 20s got me through even harder times ahead. While I knew deep in my soul that I identified with the traits of empaths and highly sensitive people, I was still afraid to embrace them fully - to be seen, to be vulnerable.

I was healing and learning so much, but there was still some unprocessed trauma in my body. I was still engaging in behavioral patterns that were not healthy and encouraged false core beliefs that were holding me back. As Bessel van der Kolk explains, "the body keeps the score." My body developed food allergies and adrenal fatigue. When I was thirty-four, I was diagnosed with PTSD and began having joint pain that made it hard to work.

Because depression hijacks your brain and makes you feel like your loved ones would be better off if you were dead, that you are a burden to them, I considered a bleak alternative. But I couldn't bring myself to leave my dog. He was the only soul I truly trusted and felt completely safe around. I know now this is because the trauma I experienced was relational in nature, and I didn't feel safe to really *be* with other people, even those who loved me very much. I couldn't bear the thought of leaving my sweet soul companion or putting him through any discomfort or pain, as I knew he was as attached to me as I was to him.

So, I pushed myself to keep going. I tried a new medication, more therapy, some hypnotherapy, and meditation. I took things step by step, finding gratitude for the peaceful, joyful moments. I made progress in my professional life, financial status, and emotional well-being. I began to feel hopeful again. Still tired and achy in body but determined and positive in spirit.

A few months later, in July of 2019, my aunt, whom I loved dearly, passed on to another dimension, and the month after, my dog left his body as well. It felt that no matter how hard I tried, I couldn't catch a break.

This was a thought pattern I had adopted, and because I believed it, I continued to attract things into my life that made my life harder, that brought me more suffering. Certainly, it wasn't my fault that these souls had passed, but I didn't have to continue being a victim. As they had many times before, my earth and celestial angels stepped in with an after-death communication from my dog. His message gave me the strength to carry on and tap into my warrior spirit once again.

In the past year, thanks to a lot of inner work, I find myself fully inhabiting my body more than ever before. Although I still get out of balance, I feel better in my physical body than I think I ever have. I use my yoga practices of asana, meditation, and breathwork to keep me centered. I apply what I've learned from trauma-focused therapy daily, hour by hour, minute by minute sometimes. I listen to music that matches my mood to help me process what's coming to the surface to be healed.

I spend time in nature, connecting with animals and prioritize time alone to cleanse my energy after being around a lot of people. I use water, crystals, essential oils, and herbs to bring myself back to balance. I let myself feel and cry a lot. I make a conscious effort to come into the present moment and connect to my own true energy. I do my best to get enough rest and honor what I feel in my body with regards to that. I journal often and express my feelings to others I trust.

I continue to read and study energy, trauma, yoga, and spirituality to gain perspectives and ideas and apply what resonates. I hold compassion for myself and let things go on my to-do list, reminding myself often that I am always safe and protected. I connect to the frequency of peace when I feel overwhelmed or afraid, and I talk to my inner child about what she is feeling at the moment. I allow myself to zone out and detach if I need a mental break.

I think it's noteworthy that I have experienced some significant traumas in my life, which have no doubt played a part in my story. Still, I do believe that another piece of the puzzle, perhaps even why I was affected by the trauma the way that I was in the first place, is the fact that I identify as an empath. I feel things deeply. It's not always pleasant, but I have learned to find peace even in the pain. Even after seeing the darkest of the darkness, I believe that every soul on this planet is a piece of God, the universe, something greater and more amazing than our human brains can even fathom. Maybe we all chose a part to play before we incarnated? I still haven't figured it all out yet, and maybe I never will in this human form.

What I do know is that empaths have the power to heal ourselves and live fully and freely. That is actually what we came here to do! Pain is temporary and will pass. Suffering is due to attachment.

We are so much more powerful than we are taught to believe with regards to detaching from pain and living in love even in the midst of chaos and discomfort. Believe in yourself. Validation from others is important but only lasts so long. You have an infinite supply of unconditional love inside of you. Offer that to yourself. Knowing yourself, your patterns, your likes, your dislikes, your feelings, and your beliefs is part of the journey. I don't know why some of us are more sensitive than others, but I do know that denying this truth or making yourself feel bad about this fact is not helpful. We are all different, and that is a marvelous thing!

It can be a difficult journey as an empath because we usually go through some pain to learn how to manage our gifts. These days I know how to work with my thoughts and tap into energy to shift how I am feeling. The positive frequencies feel out of this world amazing! When I meet people, I sense their energy right away, all of their light and darkness. I can feel what they are feeling. This is a powerful tool, especially as a healer. It helps me to tap into what people want me to see but may not say.

There is nothing "wrong" with you,
and there never was.

Being able to sense people's needs and wants is certainly an asset, but it's important to stay somewhat detached, too. This feels uncomfortable to an empath at first, of course, but it is so helpful. It's important to remember you can be compassionate and still hold your own frequency. I actually think this is a big part of the empath's journey here on Earth. I know this is hard work. It can be especially challenging if you have experienced any kind of abuse or neglect in childhood because oftentimes, we learn to be caretakers in order to survive.

We all have our own journey, and your needs are important too! You must be your own best advocate. You must listen to the wise voice inside. You must listen to your body. When you learn to balance these things, you become a superhero. I am still learning and practicing, but I have had moments so beautiful that I know it's true, and it is why I choose to stay here on Earth. To quote Krishna Das, "My god is real, for I can feel him in my soul."

We are pieces of stardust living in these human forms.

We are both primitive and divine, human and God. Our journey is to balance the two, and when we do, we will find heaven on Earth. It starts within yourself. You must find peace inside first. People have hurt you, but trust me, it was all to make you stronger and love even deeper. It was never about your worth, only their own struggle.

Empaths have a well of strength and resilience. Opening your heart even in the face of fear is true courage! You can transform your pain into power and do great things. There is nothing "wrong" with you, and there never was. Nature doesn't make mistakes. You are part of nature. You are here for a reason. Humanity needs you; you matter beyond words. You are worthy of living fully in your human form and becoming "real." The truth is, "life" doesn't get better, but *you* do.

Alyce Martin is an alignment-focused yoga teacher and usui/holy fire reiki master. She loves being outdoors, spending time with animals, meditating, baking, cooking, creating, dancing, singing, snowboarding, and hiking with her Australian cattle dog. Alyce aspires to become a licensed professional counselor specializing in trauma. Her dream is to build a trauma recovery wellness center designed to support the whole person in a holistic way, incorporating yoga, meditation, therapy, bodywork, nature therapy, and reiki.

Out of the Zen and into the Fire
By Kimberly Nice

I recall my first five years of life as a fairytale. I've come to know how much pain and turmoil was swirling around me, but I was oblivious to it back then. Blissfully oblivious. Spending my days making mud pies for the fairies, communicating telepathically with a beautiful dog named Lady, and discovering magical portals in the retention ditch next to my grandmother's apartment building was my life. My grandfather listened intently as I chattered on about the beings he called my imaginary friends.

My experience after age six was difficult. Undiagnosed learning disabilities and being raised by parents who were dealing with their own pain proved to be a disastrous combination. I started using alcohol and drugs regularly at age eleven to numb my pain. I was pregnant and married before being legally able to have a cocktail.

Looking back, the birth of my first child probably saved my life, as pregnancy curtailed my alcohol use. Divorce, a second child, a second marriage to an alcoholic, and another divorce followed in rapid succession. Suffice it to say there was enough pain and sadness to bury even the most profound spiritual gifts and abilities.

By age forty, I was safely ensconced in the unconditional love of my third marriage. My guides and guardians decided it was time to stop offering gentle nudges towards a spiritual reawakening and utilize physical and mental pain to break me open. I was incredibly stubborn and pushed back. The dance started with a pill to manage stress.

Life gradually filled with medical appointments, pill bottles, and a quest for a diagnosis. Within a few years, the powers that be whittled the forest of symptoms down to the labels of Bipolar II, Chronic Lyme Disease, Generalized Anxiety Disorder, Fibromyalgia, and Ankylosing Spondylitis.

The good news was my physical and mental state of disease could be managed with a few drugs. Nineteen prescription medications and a weekly injection, to be exact. There were bright spots here and there but no lasting periods of wellness. My condition was eventually managed into a body weighing 420 pounds and loss of the ability to walk without mobility aids.

My husband often spoke about selling the home we worked so hard to buy because I could no longer navigate the steps safely. I lost the desire to make eye contact with my loved ones because all I could see was their worry over my deteriorating condition. I never considered actively ending my life but was definitely disappointed when my eyes opened some mornings. My therapist labeled that feeling as being passively suicidal. I lived this way for years.

One morning I woke up feeling different. I realized, for perhaps the first time in my life, that I had free will. Not the smoking, drinking, self-destructive free will but the much bigger aspects of it. Could I choose to be well instead of sick? I figured I owed this theory at least the benefit of an experiment. I chose to take my pain medication only when I truly felt physical pain.

Then I chose to sit with the pain for a bit and, in a way, asked it to teach me.

Was it exacerbated by stress or certain activity? Did rest help? I now understand this was the process of me coming back into my physical body. I thought about going into an elaborate explanation of coming back into my body, but I trust that your favorite internet search engine will answer any questions on the topic.

This unintentional mind over matter lifestyle I began living quickly manifested into a part-time independent sales job. I was overjoyed to be earning money again after depending on my husband to provide for my every need for so many years. Within months this position afforded me the chance to travel to a women's empowerment retreat and assist with a presentation on self-love and body positivity.

Everything about this trip scared me. How would my broken body respond to a ten-hour car ride? How would my canes, compression stockings, and pill bottles be received at a wellness retreat? How could I encourage others to love themselves when I hated who I'd become?

Despite the fear, I said yes to the opportunity. Weeks leading up to the trip were filled with attempts to ready myself for hiking, yoga, and the other activities on the retreat itinerary. Interestingly enough, there was one aspect of the trip that didn't frighten me at all. There was a fire walk scheduled for the final evening.

How hysterically odd it was that yoga frightened me but walking across hot coals didn't evoke so much as a goosebump of anxiety.

You see, the years of untreated Lyme Disease caused severe neuropathy in both of my feet. It had become so debilitating that I would fall over if I closed my eyes while standing. Neuropathy meant no fear of feeling my feet burn.

The road trip went well, and I arrived in the beautiful sanctuary of the Smoky Mountains, no worse for the wear. I met a beautiful group of kind women, many of whom remain my dearest friends. I began to see my flaws as stepping stones to growth. I used my cane for support during hikes and yoga, but I was fully participating in the retreat! My body was actually amazing me!

Morning meditation replaced my rescue meds for anxiety, and fresh mountain air reduced my need for narcotic pain relief. The final evening in Tennessee arrived, and I found myself helping to build the big fire that we'd all be walking across. The cedar wood we carried was a beautiful reddish-brown color and had an intoxicating aroma.

I felt connected to the wood, the women, the earth, and to my body. The flames were intense. We held space for each other as we released fear, pain, rage, and limiting beliefs into the fire. We sat in a circle and sang, chanted, and drummed until our vibrations were heightened and the coals were ready for walking. I stepped up to the fire's edge without fear. The woman leading the ceremony informed me that my cane wouldn't be able to accompany me across the coal bed as the rubber bottom would melt.

I felt panic start to bubble up but instinctively used my breath to blow the fear out of my energy field. Dropping my cane in faith, I took the first steps across the fire.

*If you choose to close your eyes and
dream it into reality, you too will be
led across your own healing fire.*

Reaching the center of the coal bed, I could feel the warmth and crackling embers under my feet. The blades of grass tickled my toes as I stepped out of the fire. I remember sobbing with amazement over regaining feeling in my feet! I walked across the glowing coals seven times that night and abandoned my cane in a metal recycling bin as we left the mountains in our rear-view mirror. I haven't experienced neuropathy nor used a cane since that night.

It would be lovely to leave you with that happily ever after ending, but alas, true healing is a spiral. Life since feeling the fire has been full of blessings, lessons, victories, and heartbreak. I've lost relationships I considered to be lifelong and rock-solid, while others I assumed permanently damaged have healed. I've realized dreams, witnessed them shatter, only to reveal a more beautiful dream to realize. There has been healing of my physical body that has confounded the medical establishment. Yet,

I've come to understand that physical pain is a sleeping dragon that occasionally wakes to teach me and guide my journey.

I've danced with and ultimately overcome my dependence on narcotics. It wasn't willpower that afforded the victory. It was an understanding that pain is one of my greatest teachers, and numbing the discomfort only prolonged the inevitable lessons. A significant and almost effortless 150-plus pound weight loss is also worth mentioning.

It wasn't a specific diet or exercise plan that brought me towards a healthier weight. It was awakening to the fact that for me, excess weight was a powerful layer of protection both physically and energetically. If people were busy judging my obesity, they would leave my much more vulnerable emotional wounds alone. As my spirit was healed, the pounds fell away. It still blows my mind that I harbored wounds that required me to carry around the weight of an average human as protection!

These realizations and recovery fueled my need to explore many alternative healing and metaphysical modalities. My life's work has become assisting others in navigating their soul healing and life lessons through reiki, hypnosis, ancient shamanic practices, spiritual counseling, and creative expression. This work continues to heal me as well, and I am perpetually amazed at how each individual's healing ripples out into the collective.

As I submit these words for publication, I will once again be face-to-face with the powerful healing of the fire. Completing fire walk facilitator certification training is the culmination of this leg of my adventure and a seemingly natural conclusion to this story. If you choose to close your eyes and dream it into reality, you too will be led across your own healing fire.

Kimberly Nice is a master energy work practitioner, intuitive, minister, QHHT facilitator, advanced illness doula, teacher, and spiritual counselor. She is devoted to assisting clients in clearing away the weeds of trauma, thus creating a more balanced and joyous life.

It is Kim's belief that each individual possesses the keys to unlocking their own wholeness. She channels multiple types of reiki/light energies and draws from shamanic traditions during session. Kim has experienced profound physical and spiritual breakthroughs during her journey of self-discovery; including spontaneous healing of illnesses and a 155-pound weight loss. Find her online at GentleArrowEnergyHealing.com.

A Golden Invitation to Allow True Compassion
By Dr. Nicole Bailey, D.C

Alchemist and Liberator of Joy

Part I: Flawed Thinking: You Get to Choose Heaven or Misery

Your vibrational signal determines your experiences... the Universe will always respond to the vibrational signal you're emitting. -Sylvie Olivier

We are all born with a unique gift. Mine is joy. I'll tell you later how I know that, but for now, it helps to know that we very often explore the exact opposite of our gift in our lifetime until we fully wake up. I was born into struggle, pain, abandonment, effort, limits, and resistance and raised to continue buying into the biggest lie that most humans buy into -- victimhood. I just thought I was given a set of circumstances to overcome, push through, bury, suppress, and conquer.

Ultimately, I thought I needed to develop a thick skin and persevere, roll up my sleeves, and do whatever it took to be successful. I was also born highly sensitive and while developing a thick skin and protecting myself with an invisible suit of armor worked for a while, it eventually came to a point where all the pushing and striving simply wasn't a match for me anymore. This looked like all kinds of things in the medical world, full of diagnoses, labels, and more limits. In other words, more effort, more overcoming, and more grief.

The Universe is wonderful at reflecting back to us the limits we are holding.

My Story:

I had a very traumatic childhood that left me with painful emotions that I thought were in my past. I thought I dealt with it. I know now that trauma can be experienced differently by different people. The trauma in my life was mostly emotional trauma. The emotional trauma was due to immediate family members being emotionally and physically unwell and both drug- and alcohol-addicted.

My biological father and my mom divorced when I was a year old. She told me that things changed once I was born and that he was jealous of me and would not take care of me. We had an on-and-off relationship until I was around eight years old when he decided he no longer wanted a relationship with me for reasons he never told me.

My mother soon found and married another man who would become my stepfather. He was a drill sergeant in the Marine Corp. and died when I was in seventh grade from the effects Agent Orange had on his heart. He was not my blood but said that he loved me like I was, and I think I felt that he did when I was young. He was also severely injured from PTSD after he served in Vietnam and beat my mother at night while she hid my brother and me in our rooms.

My mother divorced him the first time when I was in second grade, remarried him shortly after, and then divorced him a second time due to his abusive tendencies and alcoholism. At the time of his death, we had more of a relationship than my biological father and I had, but it was still random and occasional.

My brother, who is seven years older, soon developed a serious drug and alcohol problem that kept him in and out of rehab and jail into his late forties. I witnessed my mother enable him during this time, mostly unconsciously. It was clear that she felt like she was responsible for his choices. Her fear of failing as a parent was palpable without her saying a word.

I decided that I would be the "good" kid for her, and I was rewarded with words of praise when I acted the part. I felt myself being molded into perfectionism from a young age while always seeking approval and doing the thing I thought would yield the biggest return -- love.

When I was eight, my mother found the love of her life, who was diagnosed with late-stage leukemia and died before they were to be married. She left me with my grandmother for a year while she was with him in the hospital in another state. This was right after a man broke into our home, and my mother shot him. I was the one who answered the door that night. The man knocked to see if anyone was home before he would later enter.

I have repeated that conversation in my head over and over, trying to see if I could have prevented what would happen. My mother shot him as he lunged for my grandmother. He fell down the stairs clutching his chest just as 911 got there and saved his life.

I witnessed the entire thing from start to finish, and the nightmares and other effects were nonstop. I was constantly worried he would come back for me and felt like I had no one to protect me, as both my mother and brother were gone. I could not sleep in the dark, had constant nightmares, and started having stomach aches, headaches, and other anxiety-related symptoms.

When my mother came back from the hospital where her boyfriend died, she was never the same. She was distant, unavailable, and clinically depressed. My mother was always looking for someone to love her and proceeded to marry and divorce four different men four more times before I turned sixteen.

Needless to say, the bullying that ensued in my high school years was par for the course. The other kids could smell the victim on me and acted accordingly. The cherry on top was when five girls attacked me before class one morning leaving me bruised and bloodied.

My formative years were riddled with stress and loss. But I held it all together so tightly in a beautifully wrapped box with a shiny bow that no one knew, not even me. Yes, I knew what I experienced during my childhood was not like most of my peers, but I thought nothing more of it. I got to be a master at not feeling anything that was uncomfortable, either through ignoring it, suppressing it with the busyness of achieving, or always looking at the bright side, which can be one way the mind tricks us into not feeling.

I was living the dream, or so I thought. I had a wonderful family, a loving partner, three amazing and healthy children, a successful business, great friends, and I enjoyed nice vacations. It was way more than I ever grew up with, and I measured this as success.

Flawed thinking was at the root of my lifelong relationship with victimhood. I didn't realize that the information my body was giving me through my emotions and what my life was showing me in my reality were gifts just waiting to be discovered. I didn't even have to dig for them either -- The Universe just put them right in front of me.

It was simple, but here I was making it hard because I had a belief that life was hard, that I needed to work hard to prove myself worthy and to love myself.

I was identifying with what I saw in the physical -- in my life, in my body, and making it mean something about me that wasn't true at all about who I really am. I was placing my attention on what I could see with my physical eyes and feel in my physical body. However, what we see in the material is only 0.00001% of what's actually here. I was giving my power to a falsehood and perpetuating the victim complex.

Yes, it's true that what manifests in the physical is created from the non-physical, the 99.9999%, but I had no working knowledge of this truth. I was strictly using my cognitive mind to make all the decisions, which put me and my life into a chronic survival pattern -- a fight or flight rollercoaster full of adrenaline. Sound familiar? – it's the American way -- even the American dream.

We aren't taught that we are infinite, powerful co-creators with the Universe or that the results of this creation with the Universe is in direct correlation with our vibrational signal, which we are emitting at all times from our energy field.

Once we realize this, we step out of the victimhood dance and everything that comes with it, and we move toward our authentic place of power from within -- which is our true nature.

It is from this place of deep connection to ourselves that we can truly honor all of our experiences. It also allows us to see what was created in the past and even what's currently showing up in our reality as just that -- an experience. We can always choose to consciously create, resulting in an outcome that is more aligned with who we are rather than running on autopilot.

In my former life experience, when I moved through life as an empath that felt others' emotions as my own, I was consistently overwhelmed. I thought it was my job to make sure everyone was having fun, happy, getting what they needed, feeling good, feeling supported, etc. I was the do-gooder that always put myself last - again because I was unconsciously seeking love from the outside.

Also, I was judging their experience as bad or not good enough. I found myself feeling sorry for most people. I was seeing their experience through my own patterns and beliefs, otherwise known as mental archives and crystallized emotions. This kept my vibrational signal, which is invisible, at a very low frequency.

Of course, I thought something was missing in my life and proceeded to effort through it. What I was manifesting was what most people deem respectable and successful -- a loving family and a successful business. However, my life was not without sacrifice. It required enormous amounts of work.

Feeling others' emotions as my own is not a habit that can be supported long-term, especially when my job involves caring for hundreds of people on a weekly basis. I was buying into another big lie -- that other people need to be protected -- that I needed to be protected.

All I needed to do was remember who I was in the first place and stop interfering with others' experiences. This would be the healing that was required -- for me as well as those seeking my healing abilities.

Part II: Moving from Inspiration, Not Desperation: Clarity, Fluidity, and Lightness

Life is the dancer; you are the dance. -Eckhart Tolle

My mentor, Sylvie Olivier of Golden Heart Wisdom, calls this "inhabiting one's space." She's also the one who let me know what my unique gift is.

Being able to occupy or inhabit my space is my foundation.

In order for all the other pieces of wholeness to naturally align the way they were designed to, being in my own space is imperative. Inhabiting my own space invites others to do the same, both unconsciously and consciously. They align with themselves almost like a mirror neuron effect, but beyond that.

This has been one way I'm able to assist those around me through massive shifts toward more wholeness. Previously, I could not do this on the scale I am now because I was buying into the limit or the story of the person I was assisting and feeling sorry for their pain. Being highly sensitive, I was over-caring while trying hard to make it go away as fast as possible.

*It becomes clear that the only responsibility
we have in life is to connect deeper to
ourselves and to allow our essence to shine
and ripple into the world for all of humanity
to see and feel.*

I was taking on their delusion, feeling it in my energetic and physical body, which can't ever work for anyone involved. This is usually the story of the empath. In other words, I was not solid in my natural ability to co-create in alignment with my heart and true self.

Remembering my wholeness was the best decision I ever made. It allowed me to access a bliss-like state and to feel profound peace -- to be free of the effects of mental archives and crystallized emotions. Now, when others are in my presence - whether it's friends, family, or my practice members - they are able to receive healing just by who I am.

I witness and get to co-create bigger health and emotional healings and life transformations much more often and more simply. I am no longer trying to fix someone - simply honoring who they really are. It is in this deep honoring that the vibrational frequency of the person raises to the degree required to dissolve lower densities, which keep pain and illness in place.

By holding a space of true compassion for another, heaviness cannot exist. In the dismantling of heaviness, a person has the opportunity to remember who they really are and become truly free. Even remembering a small amount of this inherent wholeness fuels vitality, which leads to even more of life's sweet gifts, like harmony with self and personal relationships, and prosperity, in all of its forms.

This is the place we access where life is really fun. It is here that we live in connection to our deepest and truest self, full of abundance with access to all of life's resources. This is beyond deserving, as it is our natural birthright as human beings.

Once we stop identifying with all the parts of victimhood, the victim, the bully, and the savior, we recognize and remember that we are made of pure love.

The veil over our eyes begins to lift. We begin to see with clarity. The doubts start to fall away, and, in their absence, comes true freedom.

It becomes clear that the only responsibility we have in life is to connect deeper to ourselves and to allow our essence to shine and ripple into the world for all of humanity to see and feel. This process happens through us, for us, and for humanity, if we are willing.

The cycle of creating unconsciously from mental archives and crystallized emotions ceases as we align to the light within us and everyone else. With that, the heavier densities of effort, control, lack, expectation, and limits within the vibrational signal simply no longer exist.

Once we remember the power of clarity and our part in conscious creation, fluidity follows. Fluidity invites ease, comfort, joy, and peace to emanate. Effort and struggle in any form transmute into a natural flow and rhythm. This softening allows for lightness. This lightness is very palpable in our moment-to-moment experience.

Part III: Welcome Home: Accessing the Wisdom of the Heart & Intelligence of the Body Through Compassion

What if you slept And what if

In your sleep You dreamed And what if

In your dream

You went to heaven

A GOLDEN INVITATION TO ALLOW TRUE COMPASSION

And there plucked a Strange and beautiful flower And what if

When you awoke

You had that flower in

Your hand

Ah, what then?

-Samuel Taylor Coleridge

If we as humans are powerful co-creators, then why are so many suffering? The simple answer is that those who are suffering don't know the truth of who they are and that they get to choose. We choose by accessing the wisdom of the heart, the part of us that is infinite, and by seeing through the mental archives and crystallized emotions.

The heart is infinitely compassionate and does not judge. It holds the space for peace, unattached to any outcome, yet still holding space for the highest opportunity of expansion for all.

The body is our bridge to our creativity. Feeling too much is usually the way the empath operates. However, feeling too much is not a "problem." It is the judgment of what we feel that literally turns to poison.

As a chiropractor, I get to see firsthand all kinds of things that people create in their bodies when in judgment. I also get to see how quickly things shift once they become conscious. The body is inherently healthy and full of vitality and responds to us being connected to our heart, even just a little.

This is how we truly nourish and heal all parts of us and those around us. This is the real *essence of vitality,* which can only come if we choose to act from a place of true compassion. Compassion comes from the heart, while empathy comes from the mind. Choosing to see all experiences as serving the highest good of all involved without judgment puts all of us in a place to facilitate the remembrance of who we really are.

The most amazing piece is that this is when life is most joyful and fun and effortless. The irony is that as a chiropractor, I talk about alignment and posture to most people, but now those terms take on an entirely different meaning and vibration.

My own liberation of joy happened when I stopped being scared of life, living from fear, making fear-based choices, and started to realize I was the powerful pilot in charge of the ride I was on. It turned out that most of my life was lived from fear, so I had a lot of opportunities for joy to be liberated.

As a chiropractor who is deeply steeped in the innate wisdom and intelligence of the body, I never really listened to my body's own signals or dare let them be heard. I never really connected to myself or my body in the way that was required for the alignment of true freedom.

In hindsight, I did not know how to really listen to the signals and messages my body was giving me. I was not letting myself access this superpower because it was too painful from a subconscious perspective. Once I became aware and became in tune with the messages from my body, my life started to flow with true ease, profound joy, harmony, vitality, and prosperity.

This is the kind of freedom we are all sensing is our birthright, but that we are going about in a very roundabout way, full of twists and sometimes treacherous turns. Our intuition of the body knows how to steer us in the direction that is our true north -- our *joy*! This is your invitation to remember who you really are.

I feel truly inspired and called to play with uncovering and rediscovering joy. This is the gold within that makes all things possible. -- Dr. Nicole Bailey

Dr. Nicole Bailey has been serving her community for the last twenty years. She assists the healing process through the direct rediscovery of one's pure essence. She knows that an entirely new reality is available within the wisdom of your own heart. Her purpose is to allow the wisdom of the body to sublimely shine and emanate harmony. She offers her healing services both in-person and remotely. Find her online at:

www.drnicolebailey.com and on Facebook and Instagram @drnicolebailey

Feeling Too Much: An Open Letter to a Young Empath
By Amy I. King

Dear Young Empath,

You are magic, and I mean that. You have the unique ability to feel everything! But I imagine that you struggle to figure out where you fit in and manage things like anxiety and depression, which can significantly impact an empath. I remember in high school feeling like I never really fit in with one group of people. I flitted from one crowd to another. At one point, I was dealing with so much of other people's stuff that I became depressed. I would go for days, unable to function normally. It wasn't until I was an adult well into my 20s that I was diagnosed with anxiety and depression.

I tried every prescribed drug available and have found methods other than drugs that work for me. Don't fret! You are a member of a large and growing community. Years ago, when I was young, the word empath was not commonplace. Now, it's everywhere, and we are everywhere. I want to take this opportunity to impart some wisdom to make your journey a bit smoother.

Give from your saucer, not from your cup.

You feel every single thing so intensely, which will exhaust you. When you go to a party, you will feel everyone at that party. You will feel both the good and the bad. Small talk is not your thing, so find like-minded people and have a great time! Make sure that you get plenty of downtime in between social engagements. Relaxation is key. Clear your energy with sage, and make sure to meditate.

You will tend to put the needs of everyone else before yours. I was in conversation with a good friend and fellow empath last week. I mentioned to her the title of my favorite childhood book. I shared with her that the story was about a tree that gives everything until it is nothing but a stump. That was a lightbulb moment if ever there was one. I was emulating that book for my entire life by giving to the point of having nothing left for me. Giving until you have nothing can cause you a great deal of emotional pain.

FEELING TOO MUCH : AN OPEN LETTER TO A YOUNG EMPATH

Please, put your needs first. It is not selfish; it is responsible and necessary. You are indeed your first responsibility.

Give from your saucer, not from your cup. Others can have the spillover. You have a strong belief in humanity and want to believe that everyone is innately good. The truth is, most people are. However, I have dug more people out of holes than I can recall, and none of those people are in my tribe today. Those people are the users. They will use you until you stop giving, and then poof, they will disappear.

That is where boundaries come in. Setting good boundaries will save you a lot of heartache and pain. Do not allow everyone to be so close to you and your personal life. Be discerning. Take your time getting to know someone before deciding whether or not they should be a friend. If someone tries to get familiar too quickly, that is a red flag. You have an unfortunate bonus. You tend to attract the narcissists of the world. It is not your fault. They feed off of empaths. You do not want that, and you do not want to commit years of your life to someone who is only using you. You will learn over time how to spot them and move on.

Once someone has become your friend, you might find that they often come to you with their problems. You are a healer. They can sense that. Listen, be compassionate, and advise, but don't take on those problems as if they are yours. I once absorbed my friend's struggle with selling their house. I was sick with worry. Why? It wasn't my house! But every time we talked; she was clearly in strife over it. I took on that emotion.

You might spend a bit too much time worrying about what others think of you. Guess what!? Most people aren't thinking about you at all. Most people are worried about what others are thinking of them. So, stop worrying about everyone else's opinions and start focusing on what will make you happy. You will be so much more fully yourself when you have the knowledge of what makes you happy. Happiness is the key to life. When my mother passed, she didn't tell me to work harder or make more money. She told me to "Be happy." Do not live your life in any way other than how you want to live it. It is yours!

You are a naturally curious person. You will probably be an avid reader. Your thirst for knowledge is tremendous. Read as much as you can and read on a variety of topics. You may find reading self-growth books focused on developing your natural abilities to be helpful and insightful.

It is likely that when someone cries, you automatically cry with them. When I was a teacher, I had a conference that involved the student, parent, and the child's other teachers. When asked why she wasn't performing to her abilities, the child began to cry. "Oh, no," I thought. I could feel the waterworks welling up, so I put my mind to anything other than that current situation. A tear fell, but I was able to keep my composure. It happens. If I see a Hallmark commercial, I will cry my eyes out. Silly, but true!

It's okay to cry with someone, but please don't pull the other person's sadness in as well! It will benefit you to learn your energy. Sit in meditation every day so that you are familiar with yourself. When you feel someone else's energy, you will discern between what is theirs and what is yours. You can keep it out of your energy field. Feel it, but don't absorb it.

Use discretion when choosing television shows or movies. You may be overwhelmed by violence in the media. Guard yourself. It's okay to skip the latest box office smash if it will trigger you. Stick to light-hearted comedy when possible.

As an empath, your environment is essential to your well-being. Clear the clutter from your space and keep it clean. Your home should rise up to greet you. A clean, well-organized home will add to your well-being.

One of the best and worst things about being an empath is seeing the truth and detecting lies. The trick is, you have to listen to it. Be still and know that you know. I knew someone lied and disregarded that feeling in the past. That's when you end up kicking yourself later because someone took you for a ride. So, listen in the beginning and save yourself some trouble.

Your ability to love is enormous. Empaths are over the top when we love someone. You may have your heart broken more than a few times. Learning to slow down has helped me tremendously. You can feel something for someone without being transparent from the beginning. Let that intimacy grow over time. The right people will love you right back with as much intensity as you give.

Whatever road you take in this life, know that you are exceptional. Treat yourself as such, and you will be able to accomplish anything. Always be gentle with yourself. You will make mistakes along the way, and that is how you learn. Take the lesson, and never beat yourself up.

I want to leave you with this: there is absolutely nothing wrong with you. Your sensitivity is a superpower. Use it wisely! There are so many of us in your corner supporting you. Go out into this world and use your gifts to live a happy life!

FEELING TOO MUCH : AN OPEN LETTER TO
A YOUNG EMPATH

Amy I King is a Certified Life Coach. She is a contributing author of international bestsellers: *Inspirations: 101 Uplifting Stories for Daily Happiness; Manifestations: True Stories of Bringing the Imagined into Reality; The Grateful Soul: The Art and Practice of Gratitude;* and *The Courageous Heart: Finding Strength in Difficult Times.* When not writing, she enjoys music, movies, art, travel, and time with loved ones. Her relationships with clients are built on trust and vulnerability. She welcomes the opportunity to work with you to help you transform your life! Email her at: yourphenomenallife585@gmail.com.

THE EMPATH EFFECT

Jake
By Holly Lozinak

For eleven years, I was fortunate enough to take a break from working in the corporate world to stay at home and raise my three sons. During those years, we had a lot of fun exploring and going on adventures. We made wonderful memories. My children, especially my oldest son Jake, were very empathetic to nature and the creatures that live there. They were always taking care of plants and animals, and Jake always watched out for his little brothers. My son Jake was a happy guy; he always wanted people around him to be happy too. He had such a contiguous laugh.

Over the years, we celebrated many birthdays, holidays, and backyard barbeques with friends and family. The years flew by. Next thing we know, Jake is learning to drive. When he came home from passing his driver's test, the first thing he did was point out that he checked the organ donor box on his license. That was an odd moment for me. On the one hand, I was proud; on the other hand, the thought of it being implemented was unthinkable.

High school years were passing fast. The summer between Jake's junior and senior years, he had his wisdom teeth removed, and the doctor prescribed Percocet for the pain.

A few years after Jake graduated high school, I was in the lunchroom at my work, and I was crying. A new employee walked in; she saw that I was upset and asked if she could help in any way. My response was, "Not unless you can help me with my son who is addicted to drugs." We talked for a little bit, and then we went back to work. The next morning the same employee came up to me and asked if I had ever heard of Padre Pio? I said, "No."

Though I was raised Catholic, I could not recall knowing about him. She told me that she had a dream that she should give me his prayer. She told me he was a very powerful saint, and this was a very powerful prayer. She told me there was a Padre Pio shrine not too far away that I could go and visit. Then she handed me a folded-up piece of paper. I said thank you and put the paper in my pocket.

Later in the evening, I had a really bad feeling about my son. Something was wrong. I texted back and forth with him a little bit, but it just didn't feel right. I was helpless; I didn't know what to do at this point in his addiction. I took the piece of paper out of my pocket and looked at the prayer. I said the prayer out loud and cried myself to sleep.

The next morning at work, I got the phone call that no parent ever wants to get. My son had overdosed. We spent the next four days in the intensive care unit by my son's side. What happened that first night changed my perspective on everything.

The first night, we walked into my son's ICU room, and he was lying with tubes, ventilators, and all kinds of machines hooked up to him. It looked really bad, but I was still hopeful. As we stood there absorbing the reality of what was happening, a few of us were by my son's side when we noticed bright red blood appearing on the white sheet under my son's left hand. I asked the nurse, "What is that? Why is he bleeding?" as I pointed to the area.

The nurse picked up his hand and turned it over. His palm was red with blood, but there was no blood on top of his hand. The nurse looked confused and said, "I'm not sure." Then she left and brought back two more nurses to check the IVs and tubes that were going into my son. They all looked baffled. They turned to us and nicely asked us if we could please wait in the waiting room while they cleaned him up. I never found out why.

Later that night, as I sat in my son's hospital room, I did some research on Padre Pio. I read he was an Italian saint known for living with a physical condition called stigmata, which is bleeding from the hands like Jesus' wounds. His stigmata first appeared on his left hand in 1918. I couldn't help but wonder if my son's unexplained bleeding from his left hand was a sign from Padre Pio? Were my prayers answered? Was my son going to be okay?

Friends and family visited the hospital over the next few days. It was good to be able to spend that time with them and hear stories about my son that I had not heard before. We laughed and we cried. One night, we had a meeting with the neurologist; he told us there was nothing else they could do for my son, and the doctor proclaimed him brain dead. They told us his license said he was an organ donor and they had limited time to find a match, so they quickly searched for organ donor recipients.

The night before he was going to be taken off of life support, still sleeping in a chair next to my son, something woke me up. I had a weird feeling, looked around, and looked up at the ceiling. It seemed my eyes were playing tricks on me. Whether it was from trauma, lack of sleep, dehydration, or shock, I sat there and watched the ceiling move and bend.

As people were hustling and bustling to prepare my son for leaving this world, it seemed that the other side of the veil was hustling and bustling to receive my son. At that moment, I felt that my son's life was not ending; it was about to begin. Like a caterpillar to a butterfly, my son was going to be reborn.

The last night, it was late; the hospital was empty, dark, quiet, and a little eerie. They were about ready to wheel my son from the ICU to the operating room. I was in his room, standing by his side with three other women; I asked them if they would sing happy birthday to my son with me. I knew I was never going to be able to sing it to him again, and now, I felt like he was having a rebirth.

When we were done singing, I kissed his forehead and told him I loved him. Then I looked at the clock on the wall. The time was 11:11 PM. At that exact moment, the nurse pulled the curtain back and said, "It's time to go."

I wanted to be there when they took him off of life support, when his heart stopped. I needed to see the flat line on the monitor. I saw him come into this world; I needed to see him leave this world. The other family members had already said their goodbyes to Jake and waited down the hall in a staff lounge. His girlfriend asked to go too. I said yes. We went into the operating room to say goodbye to my baby.

My baby, a twenty-three-year-old man well over six feet tall, lay there with a white sheet up to his chest. We only had a few minutes, so the two of us hugged, and cried over, and kissed his body. At that moment, I had a vision of Mother Mary and Mary Magdalene crying over Jesus' lifeless body. I had this overwhelming pull toward that vision, and I had a very powerful connection of oneness with them. The three of us, the three of them, two women crying over a loved one.

For the first time, I could feel her pain, her grief, and her love over the loss of a child. Then I heard the long monotone sound of a monitor in the room; I looked up, and the line was flat. I kissed my son one last time and said goodbye. The time was 12:32 AM.

We arrived home from the hospital in the early morning hours. Once we were home, I received a text from some of my son's friends. They had painted a mural in his honor and wanted to share it with us. It was amazing. My son would have been so honored. At that moment, my heart filled with love and pride for my son. He had touched so many people, and that night he saved two people's lives. They found a recipient for each of his kidneys. I was so proud.

I went to sleep, and that night my son came to me in a dream. He physically showed me how strong his addiction was. I woke up crying. The next few weeks were exhausting and a blur. People coming and going. The outreach of support was incredible. The cards, phone calls, gifts, dinners, the list went on.

---

*I know that the universal language of love
will keep us connected for eternity.*

I was blessed to have so many friends and family members that took care of my family for me while I was too distraught to deal with anything. I was just trying to survive and help my kids get through this too.

About a week after Jake's funeral, I had another vision. I was told to go to Padre Pio's shrine. I was told that I would see my son's name on a *big* sign. Big was emphasized; this would be a confirmation that my beliefs are true, that we can communicate with loved ones who have passed on. My son knew I was a believer in communicating with the afterlife, and I was hoping to hear from him.

The next day, I asked a friend to go with me to the shrine. We decided on a time and date, and I met her there. My mouth dropped open when I pulled the address up on my GPS. The street number was 111, and it was on route 100.

The shrine was beautiful. Being there made me feel at peace. We walked around the whole place. As we walked and looked around, I was continuously looking for my son's name, but I saw no sign that said Jake, let alone a *big* sign.

What I found out was why an Italian saint's shrine was out in the middle of eastern Pennsylvania. I discovered that a local woman had a daughter, who was born at Sacred Heart Hospital, with a kidney disorder. The doctor told them she would not live more than a few years. But after mother and daughter traveled to Italy, and she was blessed by Padre Pio, the daughter lived well into her 80s. I also found out that Padre Pio started bleeding from his left hand on September 20th. September 20th was my son's girlfriend's birthday, and Jake was born at Sacred Heart Hospital. The only organs he donated were his kidneys. What were the odds? Still no sign of my son's name anywhere.

As my friend and I were getting ready to leave the shrine and part our separate ways, my girlfriend hugged me and said she was so glad that I decided to meet her at the shrine. She said she was afraid the sign across the street would upset me.

I said, "Sign? What sign?"

She said, "Oh, that's right, you didn't come from that direction."

I asked again, "What sign?"

She told me that across the street was a flea market called "Jake's Flea Market!" There was a *big* sign out front that said exactly that, "Jake's Flea Market." Wow, what an incredible feeling I had at that moment. I took a deep breath and smiled. I had to go see the sign. She was right; there was a *big* sign, right across from Padre Pio's shrine, that said "Jake's Flea Market." I would say my son was sending me a sign.

When I found out that my son's girlfriend was born on the same date as the start of Padre Pio's stigmata, I knew I had to bring her to the shrine. We arranged a date, and I picked her up and drove her there one sunny Saturday morning. We walked all around the chapel and the gardens. Toward the end of the visit, we went into the museum. As we were about ready to leave, all of a sudden, we were kind of blocked by a volunteer from the museum who started loudly and theatrically telling the story of Saint Helena.

We didn't want to be rude, so we felt compelled to stay and listen to his performance. He proceeded to tell us about Saint Helena and the story of the True Cross. As he's finishing his story, he told us there is a relic exhibit in the basement of the shrine. One of the relics in the exhibit was displayed as a splintered piece from the True Cross of

Jesus. When he finished his story, we figured we might as well go check out the exhibit since it was only shown there twice a year.

The two of us followed him down into the basement and looked at all of the relics. At the end of the exhibit was an impressive display for the relic of the True Cross. The two of us knelt down on the bench in front of the relic to pray. Another vision came to me. This time, Mother Mary and Mary Magdalene were kneeling behind us and praying as well. I could feel their strength and powerful love.

The kind of love that connects everyone and everything, the kind of love that travels through space and time, the kind of love that makes us all One. I took a deep breath and exhaled, and thanked her.

The days, weeks, and months went on. Jake sent us incredible signs and came to us in our dreams. The first holidays were tough. I told my sons we would change traditions if they wanted and start something new.

It was the first Christmas Eve after my son passed; I was upstairs in my bed when I heard the doorbell ring. My kids answered the door, but I did not want to go downstairs.

A friend of the family had stopped over and brought us a cornucopia of Padre Pio merchandise. He brought us books, statues, rosaries, prayer cards, and more. Enough for each of us to have one of everything. After he left, I went downstairs; my kids wanted to show me everything on the kitchen table. His gifts were very unexpected, but we were touched by his thoughtfulness and generosity. It was time to go, and we had to get ready to leave for my sister's house to celebrate Christmas Eve.

It was late by the time we got home, but we decided to open presents. After the wrapping paper was all put in a trash bag, my boys sat there fidgeting with their new Christmas presents, I walked over, and I picked up my phone. I said to my boys, "Guess what time it is?" The time on my phone was 12:32 AM. I looked up to the heavens, and I said, "Merry Christmas, Jake! We love you, and we miss you!" I blew a kiss to my son. At that exact moment, the light hanging over the kitchen table with all the Padre Pio merchandise on it blew out, and that part of the room went dark! My boys looked at me with wide-open eyes, and I said, "That's your brother wishing us a Merry Christmas back. Love you, Honey!"

Time has passed, and years have gone by, recently it was my son's sixth year anniversary of his passing; I woke up that morning and asked my son for a sign. I went about my usual day but didn't pack a lunch before I left for work; I decided to treat myself. I went out to a local deli on my lunch break. I walked by the chip aisle and thought to myself, *Jake loved those chips; today, I will get chips in honor of Jake.* When I went up to pay for my lunch, the cashier said, "That will be $11.11!" I said, "Really?" A huge smile came across my face. I said to myself, *Hi Buddy, Thank You.* That made my day.

A lot has changed since Jake passed, but we know he would want us to be happy and live our lives to the fullest. We continue to get incredible signs from Jake, letting us know he is always around, loving us, and watching over us. Now every time the clock turns to 11:11 or a random 11:11 shows up somehow in my daily life, I say "Hi" to my son, and I know that the universal language of love will keep us connected for eternity.

Holly Lozinak is a mother of three grown sons who has been working with and teaching young children for the past twenty years. Holly is a reiki master and a lover of animals and nature. She is also an artist who has dedicated many years volunteering her talents creating murals for her local community. Holly has been experiencing 11:11 since the late 80s. She hopes to spread love, hope, and strength by sharing her experiences that surround this number.

THE EMPATH EFFECT

Finding My Joyful Self
By Cristy Joy

Happiness Life Coach & Creator of the Joyful Self
Wellness Center

As I share my journey, I realize what I thought was my story was only a chapter in my life. Who I was just five years ago is not who I am today. I also know that who I will be in the next five years is not who I am today.

The difference now in my perspective is that I am okay with change and allowing the journey to unfold. I am learning and growing much more quickly than I did in the past. Before, I needed to repeat my lessons over and over, some of them for years and years. Now, the lessons come very quickly into my life. I notice them for what they are, sit in the knowledge and feeling, and then pull up my big girl panties and be grateful for the experience.

In the past, I would obsess and over-think and over-feel every little thing. I thought I could control everything. I was prepared for every situation. If only I thought of every contingency, then I could be happy and have my happy ending.

Instead, I am now living my joyful life, in the present, with myself and those that I am blessed to have in my life at the moment. How did I gain this wisdom? Well, let me take you on my empathetic journey to a more joyful life.

I was born Cristy Joy in November of 1969 to young parents. I only have a few memories and photos of my parents and myself as they separated, and I was sad about losing my father. He decided to move away and never kept in contact, leaving me with a mother who suffered from depression. I see now that she could not give the love I needed because she was working so hard to provide and, I can only assume, did not love herself enough.

My mother did not raise me under any religion, so I did not have the foundation or knowledge of God from her. The only glimpse of God was during time spent with my grandmother. She talked of God, but it was foreign to me as a child. Although I cannot explain it fully in words, I felt guided and loved by something.

Looking back, someone was always sent to join me on my path just when I needed them. God would send best friends, surrogate mothers, and 'older sister' relationships. Knowing that I was never alone truly helped me navigate the emotional neglect from the people who were supposed to love me.

I know now that my mother suffered from depression, but as a child, you do not know exactly what it is, and all you feel is rejection. But God kept sending women to me at these moments, and it allowed me to find joy. I know that God was there all along, and it was not me controlling my world. This concept took many years to see and many lessons to work through.

It was only natural that I found unhealthy relationships with the men in my life. I was the firstborn and a nurturer or fixer; at least, that's what I tell myself as I graciously look back on my unhealthy past. I married someone like my father, just as my mother did, and I thought I would be happy when I fixed him. I know now how wrong and unhealthy that was of me.

The next twenty-four years had highs and lows. The highs were raising my four amazing children, a daughter and three sons. I threw all my nurturing spirit into them. I was a loving mother, and I did the exact opposite of what I experienced growing up. My intent was to show my children how much I loved them in my words and actions. Did I make mistakes? Absolutely, but it was coming from a pure place.

I spent twenty-four years distracted enough by caring for everyone else and not practicing self-care, and one day I woke up and realized I was unhappy. Where was my 'happily ever after?' I did not feel love, with the exception of my children.

Every single New Year's Eve, I asked the same question of God: "Can you please send love and peace into my life?" Both would elude me. It would come for a few days, but then old familiar patterns and cycles would show up. I would often ask God, "Don't I deserve love? I am a good person." I was asking God to fix the situation, but the cycle continued without change until I took the first step.

What was the "aha" moment for me? It was my forty-sixth birthday. I found myself crying on my bedroom floor. I wish I could say it was the first time, but this felt like my hundredth time. This time was different for me, though. I cried and pulled up my big girl panties again and told myself that it was the last time I was going to cry on my birthday. Something inside shifted, and I knew that it was going to be different.

It was in this forty-sixth year that I began to learn more about myself. I started to practice self-care and did a few things out of my comfort zone. Once again, I was surrounded by women helping me navigate the extreme emotions involved with releasing control and unhealthy patterns.

I soon discovered the world of an empath. It made logical sense that I was empathetic. I had the major sign: an ability to apprehend the mental or emotional state of another individual. That is the textbook definition of an empath - but you and I know that being an empath is so much more than just a neat, one-line definition.

An empath can sense and feel the emotions of others as if they are their own, and it is hard not to care for others. I have found over the years that people, even strangers, would tell me their problems as if they sensed I was a good listener.

I could actually feel the emotions of those around me. I would always put a hand on someone's arm or back when in conversation. I never realized I was doing that, and it wasn't until five years ago that I understood what I had been doing all along. It was second nature for me to comfort those around me, even total strangers.

Where had I learned this? I don't know if it was taught to me or if it was just an innate gift. I like to think that it is my mission in life to be here to listen, offer support, and comfort with my energy.

I thought my mission was to problem solve, fix, and pour love into others. Do you find yourself doing that as well?

Journaling kept me centered and showed me the red flags that I overlooked for years. The self-care and love told me that I mattered. I needed to pour love inside my heart. I planned on a long life, and I wanted to finally feel happy, content, and at peace.

As an empath, especially when you recognize this superpower you have, you will begin to shift your perspective and worldview. Some will be drawn to your light, while others will fear or even be angered by your light.

My journey the last five years was no different. People and things went quickly out of my life. I began to recognize them as unhealthy relationships with negative people. However, the most amazing people and opportunities began entering my life; I had cleared the way for better and bigger things. Just because I began to be healthier does not mean challenges did not appear, because they did. The differences this time around were my perspective and my reactions.

As an empath, there are important things to remember in order to maintain your empathetic energy. The top two are self-love and self-care, but there are several more. It is important to find your sanctuary inside. You can do this with meditation, journaling, yoga, and walks in nature. They are all wonderful ways to provide this atmosphere that allows you to heal and connect with yourself on a deeper level in your heart, your mind, and your soul. By doing this, you can maintain the positive energy within you.

You will quickly learn that it feels so wonderful to be in this frame of mind and will not accept even a portion of the things you used to tolerate. I actually crave new and exciting opportunities for growth and the 'feel good' emotions that inevitably follow. By releasing my old patterns and mindset, I've been opened to incredible opportunities. It is amazing all that starts to show up on your path when you just take that first step.

I was actively speaking to God in my car and everywhere. I literally threw my arms up in the air and told God that I was ready to serve. I had no idea what I was asking Him to bring into my life, but it has been so much more than I could have ever dreamed.

This was when I rediscovered my joy.

Literally two weeks after I set the intention that I was ready to serve, I began to receive messages from God. He was speaking to me and gave me the word 'transformation' to ponder on. This was not a word that I used in my day-to-day talk, but I sat with this word. He whispered into my heart that he was leading me to take steps toward my newly realized dream.

The dream that appeared to me was to create a safe place for others to come, be heard, be empowered, and be supported. I had no idea what this was going to look like, but I was trusting the process this time. The antagonists in my life said things that would typically hold me back, but this time it was fueling me to take the necessary next steps. I began to be fearless even though it was the scariest time in my life.

The ultimate sign appeared one afternoon when I was signing my divorce papers. I was asked to sign my full legal name, and when I started to write my first name, middle name, and last name, a voice in my head said, "You have found your Joy." Up to this day, I had never used my middle name, and that day I wrote my middle name, which is 'Joy.' This was a powerful moment and undeniably a sign from above.

I began to be fearless even though it was the scariest time in my life.

In the weeks that followed, I threw myself into personal development workshops and started working on all the things that kept me stuck in the past. I learned new ways to see the world. I began to come out of the victim role I had settled into over the majority of my life.

I began to love myself and learned that self-care was essential to finding peace and happiness. I found out that happiness came from within and not from any person or materialistic item. It was as if I was returning to who I was meant to be all along.

How did I bring happiness and healing into my life? I looked back at my life and found that I was happiest when I was a teenager listening to music. This is where I started with my healing. It was music that calmed my soul. As an empath, I feel music to my core: the lyrics, the energy, the vibrations all increase my inner joy.

During that first year of healing, I went to over thirty concerts. They were in every way my therapy sessions. It was important to have something in my life that brought me happiness; I began to dress up and plan dates with myself.

In 2017, I was rocked to my core with the passing of my greatest cheerleader and friend, Allix, and I was besieged by grief. I never felt grief like that. It was just when I thought I was on the right path. I felt like giving up and thought I was never supposed to be happy. Again, I asked God, "Why?" There were so many conversations with Him. I screamed at Him.

I felt like I did not have a reason to get out of bed, but God spoke through a friend and told me to get out of bed and find a concert now. It was 3 p.m. when she called, but I trusted this command and found myself in a seat at a concert by myself at 7:30 p.m.

I was not alone. God sat someone right by me, a complete stranger, to be with me and help me find some joy in the music. I cried, I danced, and I sang out loud that night. This one concert did not take away the grief, but it gave me joy for that evening. This showed me that even during periods of great pain, there can be great joy. The vibrations from the music were what I needed that evening. I was empty, and I needed to be filled with this energy.

Taking each day as a new day to heal, to love myself, to create healthy boundaries and relationships led to my greatest creation: my true self. God cleared the path and guided me to the right place to open my own wellness center. He had Allix, the dear friend that I had lost, speak to me one day during a meditative walk through a spiral labyrinth. I asked when I would be able to find a place and open the business I had been lovingly planning for over a year. The message I received was 'by my birthday.' I thought this was not possible since it was only three months away.

However, I trusted these words and continued to work on the plan but had nothing definite until just two weeks prior to my birthday. At this point, I was not even thinking about my birthday or any kind of celebration. After all, I was still navigating my grief.

I was driving with a good friend and saw a sign for a commercial building, so we stopped and got a bit excited. It was a great location, and the space was something ideal. When I called the realtor, it had just been sold, but he had another building that listed that day. We toured the building. It exceeded our expectations and fit perfectly into my budget.

Two weeks later, I decided to sign the papers and take the leap of faith to start my new journey when a voice in my head said, "It's your birthday!" Every time I think about this story, I am reminded of how incredible my journey has been in the last five years.

When I realized I could not control everything in my life and allowed things to enter into my world, all the magic began to happen. I began to trust and follow my empathetic heart. I had to heal that heart first and learn how to hold it and nurture it.

My biggest life lessons happened in the last five years. I navigated some very real and painful moments during this time, but I learned how to care for myself and shift my perspective. We are here on this earth for a very short time, and we need to learn to change the question of 'why' to 'why not.' Why not live our most authentic life? Why not sit in our pain and move through it? Why not step out of our comfort zone? Why not find our passion or purpose? Why not take that first step today?

I ask you, what is your 'why not?' Explore this question today and allow yourself to connect to all the joy you deserve. When you release the old and allow space for the new, then that is where all the magic shows up, and you will begin to find your joyful self!

Cristy Joy's mission as a happiness life coach and creator of the Joyful Self Wellness Center is to provide a safe space to help other empaths clear out the fears and false stories that hold them back. She empowers others to rediscover their authentic self, shift perspectives, and find their Joy! Learn more about her and the Joyful Self community at Joyfulself.com. You will learn to honor yourself, clear out the old stories, and create lasting joy in your life!

THE EMPATH EFFECT

Why Am I Different?
By Debra Buehring, RN, CMT

Reiki Master Practitioner

I am different. I was different the moment I was conceived. I was the third of four girls. All my sisters were born blonde-haired and blue-eyed. I had dark hair and brown eyes. Though we were from the same parents, we looked nothing alike.

Appearance wasn't the only way in which I was unique. While I didn't realize it yet, I was also different from other people in more interesting and profound ways.

One weekend in 2016, as my husband, Bob, and I were strolling through the expo hall at a healing festival, I felt pulled toward a particular booth with stones and crystals. Tom, the owner of the booth, called to me and placed a shiny silver stone into my hand.

Tom asked, "Are you approached by people you don't know in the grocery store, or elsewhere, to talk about personal things?" I nodded in agreement as he continued, "You have an invisible sign above your head flashing 'Empath.' People in pain sense this and approach you to unload their problems so they will feel better. You can turn off the empath sign as needed to prevent this from happening at inopportune times. The stone I have given you is hematite. As you can see, it is reflective. You can hold the stone in your hand and visualize yourself being enclosed in it like an egg. This 'turns off' the empath sign.

Wow! This was new. I had never heard my experiences explained this way before. I was familiar with empathy and being an empathetic person but didn't have a name for what made me different. It only took fifty-five years, but now I knew I was an empath.

Following this discovery, I researched what it meant to be an empath and how that affected my life. I found what would become one of the most instrumental books for me - *The Empath Survival Guide* by Dr. Judith Orloff. From this book, I gained profound insights about how and why I was different, recognizing that I was a physical and intuitive medical empath with telepathic and precognitive abilities. Armed with this knowledge, my previous experiences in life began to make sense.

As a child, I felt un-seen at times and would hide to see if anyone would notice I was missing. Often, I could be found alone, reading a book. Around the age of seven, I began experiencing physical problems: severe stomach pains, loose bowels, and pain in my legs. The tests performed never revealed a reason for my issues.

At fifteen, I met my soulmate, Bob, and within three months knew we would marry. We did indeed marry three years later and then began to have children. Our second son was born premature and unable to breathe on his own. Despite words of doubt from some friends and family members, I knew he would make it through and thrive.

As a young woman, I always had a special way with babies, being able to soothe them with my touch and presence. Once I was caring for six infants alone in a church nursery. It was mid-morning, and they were all getting tired and fussy. Starting with the baby fussing the loudest, I sat down in a rocking chair and rocked her to sleep. I continued to do this with each baby until all were sound asleep in their cribs. I later discovered that this was not a normal occurrence and, indeed, quite difficult for most people to accomplish alone.

Because of my positive experiences with babies, I began my nursing career in the Neonatal Intensive Care Unit (NICU). Working in the NICU could be stressful at times though I rarely let it affect my life. At one point, I began having vivid dreams about things going badly during work. These dreams were foreshadowing experiences that would occur during the shift later that very day. I began to dread going to work some days because of these dreams.

During this time, I had a strange sense we would be moving from our hometown of Phoenix, Arizona, in about two years. How could that be possible? We were close to both our families, happy with our jobs, and loved our life in Phoenix. A move was not part of our life plan. Nevertheless, I made preparations for a major move away from the only life we'd ever known. Within two years, Bob's career plans changed and required us to move. The move to Louisville, Kentucky, proved to be a difficult one for our family, but because I had sensed a change ahead of time, the transition was a little easier on everyone.

This move wasn't the only instance when I just "knew" about major events two years ahead of them occurring. Bob now jokes I have "two-year vision."

In the following years, I received many and varied intuitive flashes. For example, in the course of my job as a home health liaison, without a previous appointment, I often arrived at the right place at the right time greeted with, "I was just about to call you." Also, before my father was diagnosed with terminal cancer, I knew something was wrong. I had dreams foreshadowing his death and later my mother's need for help due to undiagnosed dementia.

Health issues I had experienced as a young girl continued as I got older. By the time I was in my early thirties, I felt like a little old woman getting out of bed in the morning. The lightest touch would hurt me, and most of the time, I was miserable.

Having been raised in a religious home, I believed God could miraculously heal through prayer and began praying fervently for God to heal me. It was in a time of deep meditation and prayer that I distinctly heard these words, "You are going to be healed. It will not be a miraculous healing but a slow process so that when you find your healing, you will be able to help others too."

With that message planted in my head, I began a long journey of healing physically and emotionally using alternative treatments plus changes in diet and exercise.

Being an empath is not an easy path, but there can be joy in life when we understand the reason for our uniqueness and pain.

This experience is what compelled me to become a massage therapist and reiki master practitioner. Through my practice, I was able to help heal myself and others. Yet, despite the progress I made with my healing, I still struggled with physical and emotional pain. I couldn't understand why.

Inspired by Tom's insightful words and through research and experience, I began to understand and value my intuitive gifts. I learned much of my pain was not my own and how to distinguish between my pain and others', letting go of what wasn't mine. This was not only true for physical pain but emotional pain as well.

There are times when I still have to ask myself, "Is this feeling really mine?" When I identify what isn't mine, I use cleansing and protective measures such as smudging with sage, setting intentions in my workspace and home, taking Epsom salts baths, and wearing crystals and stones which absorb or reflect other peoples' energy. I no longer ignore or dread dreams and visions but now view them as beneficial guides for my life.

Now that I understand what being an empath means, I identify others around me who are empaths. Those who already know they are empaths teach and encourage me to discover more about myself. For those who are unaware of their gifts, I find great joy in facilitating and leading them through their discovery of being an empath and developing their gifts.

Discovering what we are is the first step in understanding why we are different. Being an empath is not an easy path, but there can be joy in life when we understand the reason for our uniqueness and pain.

As an empath, we are endowed with many abilities that we can use to better our lives and the lives of those around us. When we work to set boundaries and protect ourselves, we can move forward to develop these gifts and share them with the world.

Debra Buehring is an empathic intuitive medical healer. She is the founder of Revitalizing Health, providing holistic services of therapeutic massage and reiki using altered states to help heal body, mind, and spirit. She facilitates an empath circle to reach and support other empaths on their path. Her mission is to decrease pain and suffering in the world one person at a time. Debbie is a registered nurse, certified massage therapist, and reiki master practitioner. Find her online at www.revitalizing-health.com or Facebook at Revitalizing Health.

Forever the Love of my Soul
By Debi Baldwin

Writer. Veteran. Warrior.

I was three years old, standing in our kitchen. I glanced at the phone and asked my grandmother why my mommy didn't call or come see me anymore. My grandmother responded, "I don't know. She must not love you."

It has taken me many years to begin healing from the trauma I experienced as a child. There have been tons of mistakes and poor choices along my path toward healing and accepting my true self, wholly and completely. It hasn't been a journey that has an actual destination. It is a constant work in progress. But as I look behind me now, the view is drastically different. I am grateful to finally be in a place where I can vulnerably stand in my story, own it, and share it with others in the hopes it encourages at least one other person.

As a little girl, they had described me as "too sensitive." A "crybaby." I cried easily and experienced all of my emotions passionately. My environment and the energy of others affected me profoundly. I was incredibly compassionate and empathetic. These were not qualities that were seen as "good" in my world. They were weaknesses. Problematic. Worthy of shame and ridicule. I was the target of that shame and ridicule often, usually from my grandmother. I quickly learned to hide myself, that my emotions were "bad," and that nowhere was safe. I was incredibly lonely.

"Little baby, cry me a handful"

the grandmother screeched at the little girl

hands cupped together, extending out toward the little girl's face

a look of complete disgust and hate on her face

the message clear to the little girl

who only cries harder

inaudible and unspoken cries for comfort

cries for love

none of which are offered

only condemnation

ridicule

"Little baby, look at the little baby"

the little girl is gasping for breath between her tears now

scared

heartbroken

feeling lightheaded

feeling abandoned

the room spinning

fighting for air

finally, slowly calming, fighting the last tears still slowly trickling from her eyes

understanding that crying is not allowed

not ok

The courts decided my mother was unfit when my parents divorced, and she was awarded supervised visitation only. My father was in Vietnam during the entire divorce process, and his parents represented him. They despised my mother and did everything in their power to ensure she had as little access to me as possible. My father was awarded custody, and his parents were awarded guardianship. It was 1969. I was two years old, and people were not thinking about the effect all of this potentially had on me.

My grandparents had raised three boys, and now my grandmother got the little girl she'd always wanted. She had "won." I was the prize. And I was often treated like some prize to be put on display. But prizes weren't supposed to have needs.

Within a year of living with my grandparents, my mother chose to end visitation. She was dealing with her own undiagnosed mental health issues as well as losing her only child. No one understood it was yet another trauma for me. She just stopped coming one day. No warning or explanation was ever given. My grandmother had "won" again.

I wouldn't reconnect with my mother until I was nine years old. I had no idea where she was or even if she was still alive, really. I had caught glimpses of her a couple of times over those years at places like our county fair, but my grandmother always very quickly ushered me away in another direction before I could get to my mother.

By the time I was eighteen, I had changed households seven times and experienced a mountain of trauma. Originally living with my mother and father and later just my mother, then my aunt and uncle, then my grandparents, then my father and stepmother, back to my grandparents, then with my mother and stepfather, and finally back to my grandparents.

Through all of that, the most unsafe places were with my grandparents and with my mother and stepfather. I felt completely unconnected, ungrounded, and unsafe in the world. Always I ended up with my grandparents and always the target of my grandmother's wrath.

I could never explain the pain I felt inside, being the sensitive girl that I was and having no one to reassure me, no one to nurture me, no one to tell me I wasn't just a "bad girl." Nor did I ever feel safe enough to speak on the other traumas I experienced. I didn't receive hugs, nor was I told I was loved. I escaped into music, reading, and made-up worlds in my mind. I shut down my emotions, my body, and my own needs. It was soul-crushing.

So many of my questions, experiences, and emotions were dismissed, shamed, or ridiculed by my grandmother; I could never discuss my experiences as an empath. Knowing things when you couldn't explain how you knew and experiencing things that others didn't understand was never well-received. I was always told it was my imagination, and I embraced that so strongly I learned to discount everything I experienced. I did it so well; it became subconscious. I became even more disconnected and simply existed.

That little girl who hid her whole life because she never felt safe made a powerful, pivotal turn toward real healing at the age of forty-one. I made the decision to stop looking for love outside of myself and to begin loving myself in action and not only words.

Feeling broken, and as if I were just a pinball being bounced around through life's machine, was no longer an option. Boundaries had been an unknown to me up until that point in my life. Both of my marriages had been abusive. The second one, with the physical abuse and resulting shame, was almost overwhelming. When I reached that turning point, I left that abusive second marriage with zero thought or regret and boundaries firmly in place. I swore I'd never compromise myself again.

Self-acceptance was unknown to me because I'd been conditioned to strive toward the expectations of others in order to prove myself worthy. Worthy of love, worthy of respect, worthy of good things. Mine were deep wounds, and I had no memories of a life without trauma since my trauma began so young.

Recognizing and accepting that my little empathic soul reacted to the trauma I had experienced as a child so much more intensely than some would have, was an important first step in my journey towards self-acceptance. Self-acceptance included the realization that I had nothing to prove.

There were many layers to my healing journey. Consistently putting boundaries in place was a crucial step. Shedding my victim mentality was another. I began to embrace the idea that nothing happens by coincidence and there are positive lessons we can carry forward from the worst of situations, and that if we can find those positive lessons, no experience was for nothing.

I experienced tremendous growth when I made the decision to be open to learning. I went back to college, and I expanded my framework that I based all of my worldviews upon. I began exploring yoga and eventually became a registered yoga teacher. I discovered the Japanese energy healing modality of reiki and became a reiki master/teacher.

My entire belief system shifted, and, for the first time in my life, I felt at peace with my own spirituality, and I felt truly connected to something bigger than myself. It was at this time that I discovered I was an empath and reflected on how this had affected me throughout my life, especially around the way I had experienced trauma. I discovered writing and the absolute power of standing firmly in my own story, willingly vulnerable.

I have fully stepped into who I have always been under all the layers and messages of who I was supposed to be.

I began to accept that, yes, I had been traumatized. Repeatedly. Experiencing trauma isn't a competition. There is no "someone else had it worse." I began to refuse all the messages from the years of traumatic invalidation that I had experienced. I began to claim all of myself with my empathic sensitivities, my hurts, my mistakes. I continued to step into my own power, finally sure I was worthy.

I am now able to make different choices that put me first. Nothing and no one can ever change my knowledge of my own worth. Though I am careful to protect myself, I no longer hide my emotions, my sensitivity, my opinions, or my empathic self. I have fully stepped into who I have always been under all the layers and messages of who I was supposed to be.

As an empath, I now see myself as powerful, and I understand what a gift my sensitivity truly is. I love myself in action. I do not compromise myself. I know I am worthy of all the love and goodness that this life can bring. I choose to serve others from that place of empathic power, listening and trusting when my gut tells me things I cannot explain. Logic is no longer needed as a crutch. I now stand in the knowledge that the Universe is always conspiring for my highest and greatest good at all times.

I not only survived; I am thriving! As I walk in my light, I hope to encourage others to vulnerably stand in their stories as they pursue their light, to become the forever love of their soul.

I love you

I feel it in my soul

With each thought of you

Each time I set eyes upon you

And feel the warmth and safety of your embrace

I know

My life is changing

I feel it shifting

I see the beautiful light

I feel the heat it radiates

And I know

It's been so long coming

Countless tears have been shed while I waited

Making mistake after mistake

As I searched

But finally, I have found what I've been looking for

THE EMPATH EFFECT

It is my own strength

And it is through that strength I heal

Old wounds finally only scars

No longer festering

The little girl is now safe

The teenager is no longer desperate for love

This road has been long

And the pain seemingly unbearable at times

But it was my path

The same path that eventually led me to you

There are no accidents, no coincidences

This was the path I was meant to walk

Now forever changed

Forever loving, nurturing, supporting

Forever the love of my soul

I am exactly who I have been waiting for

I am worthy

I always have been

Debi Baldwin is a writer, a veteran, and a warrior. She feels a calling to share her story of thriving after trauma with powerful vulnerability in the hopes of encouraging others as they navigate their own healing journeys. As an intuitive healer, Debi channels these gifts into her writing and is in the process of creating her own blog and preparing for future speaking and facilitation opportunities. Debi is also a published poet, a social justice advocate, a registered yoga teacher 200, and a reiki master/healer. She can be reached at Debi.Baldwin@gmail.com.

THE EMPATH EFFECT

Perpetual Disentanglement
By J.D.

I was in my late thirties the first time I heard the term empath. I stumbled across it randomly and instantly felt an extreme curiosity. I started to research it, and the information I read offered an explanation for my entire life. It was the first time I ever felt like a specific label fit me; the first time I felt I could truly understand myself. I was able to look back at my life and fit all the pieces into a puzzle that finally made sense.

No more pieces that were oddly shaped, or colored differently, or missing. Finally, everything had a logical explanation. This is a huge thing for someone who has always led from logic. I spent most of my life trying to understand the why's behind everything, and I no longer have to question why I feel so much, why I care so much, or why I seem to be so different from most people I know. I've always known that I was different. I didn't fit into anyone's boxes. I was often labeled as weird.

I never fit in—not in how I acted in general or in how I responded to the situations I experienced. There were various times in my life that I wished I could change, wished things were easier, that I was accepted—that I belonged. I was stuck in this strange dichotomy that I didn't understand. I hated being me, but I also loved being me. Even though I wanted to be normal, I was never willing to change certain things about myself, never willing to compromise on being me.

I didn't understand why I couldn't make myself be like everyone else. But I mostly didn't understand why others wouldn't accept me the way I was.

When I think about my earliest memories as a child, I can clearly recognize signs of social anxiety and extreme sensitivity. I longed to participate in life the way I observed others doing. Most of the time, my initial attempts to do so were in vain. Thankfully, I've always had an awareness of the strength contained in my soul.

If I wanted something, deep down truly wanted it, I was eventually able to control my emotions and feelings enough to get to have that experience. I vividly remember being about two years old and begging to get my ears pierced.

I was so excited to be told that I could. However, when we showed up, and I sat in the chair, the worker refused to pierce my ears without me verbally telling her that I wanted it done. As badly as I wanted it, I could not make myself say any words to her.

We left without getting my ears pierced. I cried. My parents agreed to take me back if I was going to tell the lady that I wanted my ears pierced. So, we went back, and I said what I needed to and left happy with my first set of earrings. This situation played out similarly in almost every new activity I tried. I was constantly overwhelmed in any new situation, especially when it involved other people.

When I started school, I was made fun of for being sensitive. I learned to numb myself to most of my emotions in order to get others to leave me alone. Extreme emotions would still make me cry, but I was able to avoid feeling them in most public situations, so that was good enough for me at the time.

The majority of my childhood was spent dealing with neglect and emotional abuse. All of my physical needs were always met, and my childhood wasn't horrible, but I can't remember a time when I didn't struggle to feel like I mattered, like I was loved, like I was even seen.

The foundation for self-worth and belonging was never formed because my parents were dealing with their own damage. They did the best they could with what they were given, and even though I somehow understood this at an early age, my emotional health was the collateral damage.

I developed a soft spot for other people's pain because I never wanted anyone else to ever feel unloved or like they didn't belong. When I was 13, I was molested. I tried to tell someone, and it basically got ignored. After that incident, I started to believe that my feelings didn't matter and I wasn't important to anybody. Nobody looked out for my well-being. No one was in my corner.

Over the next decade or so, I experienced several incidents of sexual harassment. I never reported any of it because I didn't think anyone would do anything about it. All of these experiences conditioned me to put other people's feelings ahead of mine. I spent my early adulthood consenting to things I didn't want for the simple reason that I considered their feelings first.

In my late twenties, I finally found an amazing counselor. I had tried a couple before her, and they were patronizing and condescending. I had almost given up on trying to find someone, but I had recently lost a couple of important people in my life, so I was willing to try one last time. Thankfully, she was completely different. She listened and validated every single one of my feelings. I didn't see her for long, but her sessions triggered a slow and steady positive change that lasted for years.

A few years later, I started to recognize and build on my self-worth. I started to see the flaws in a lot of the ways I thought. I began to see the beauty in some of my traits, mostly in my sensitivity and resiliency. I started to see things I liked and was proud of when I looked in the mirror. It felt great to start removing some of the weight from my shoulders. It felt even better to have some good self-esteem.

By my mid-thirties, I was starting to recognize the people in my life that exhibited toxic behaviors. At first, I made excuses for them based on their history. I found that if I accepted any of their toxic behavior, the toxicity and drama would increase. So, I started to speak up about it and removed myself from the situations where that behavior was happening.

Eventually, I saw I needed to set stronger boundaries around these people. I knew if they didn't respect those boundaries, I would have to remove them from my life. There were two people I had close relationships with that I realized were narcissists.

One of them got cut out of my life quickly after she tried to minimize the trauma in my past and basically told me that it didn't happen the way I said it did. I was dumbfounded at her attempts to minimize what happened to me and at her overall callousness.

It took me longer to recognize the situation with the second person because of the nature of the relationship. There was emotional abuse present that I took a long time to ascertain. I had known for years that I didn't like the way I was feeling but blinded myself to the reasons why.

One day, I had an epiphany and suddenly realized that he was the cause. I finally saw that I had been absorbing his energy and adapting it into my life. I was acting in a way that wasn't true to my nature, and it was causing me to feel depressed.

I spent months releasing his energy and trying to talk to him about the situation, but every time the talks fell on deaf ears. About six months later, I had had enough and started to remove him from my life.

Removing these people from my life catalyzed my healing process. Everything started moving so much faster. I was constantly stumbling across new information that increased my understanding of my experiences. I realized that all the situations I had been through were no longer things that I had to deal with, that I was able to heal from them. I understood that going through them gave me a power that not everyone could claim.

*Finding your own worth gives you a power
that no one else can ever take from you.*

I saw I had the power to know what others in similar situations are going through, the power to help them see that they can also heal, the power to show them that they are not alone. This time was also when I found out about empaths. It finally made sense to me why I allowed others to treat me so poorly in the past and why I was always so uncomfortable around crowds.

Literally, every aspect of me finally made sense in my head. Once I understood the why, it was so easy for me to implement changes that not only expedited my healing but also kept me from absorbing as much from my environment. This was life-changing. I stopped searching outwardly for all those things that we should be giving to ourselves.

I began to love myself unconditionally. I forgave myself for always being so hard on myself and for not knowing what I didn't know. I started to transform my life into one where I could easily find peace. I still have a long way to go with my transformation, but I am so far from where I started. My life before was living with whatever was dealt to me and tolerating the routine of what we are supposed to do as adults.

Now, I am building my life by doing things that bring me happiness and getting away from what is considered normal. I am not normal. I have never been, and I don't want to be. I am unique, and I have a lot to offer by being completely me. We all have a lot to offer by being completely ourselves.

Shifting my perspective around experiences and people's behaviors was the biggest help in my healing process. The healing process is lifelong and far from easy, but it is well worth everything you gain. Finding your own worth gives you a power that no one else can ever take from you, a power that we all should embrace. As much as our reality may try to convince us differently, we are never alone.

We may have to search long and hard to find them, but there are others out there who are just like us. Don't ever dim your magic because others don't understand it. Start believing in what makes you special, and don't be ashamed to let it shine. Don't let being different discourage you from being you.

Use your differences to your advantage. Changing your perceptions will allow you to untangle yourself from the burnt-out social constructs we deal with today. One day, everything will be better for all of us. Hold that hope.

J.D. is an analytical free-thinker that uses experience along with research to gain understanding in order to update her perspective on life. She is a scientist with a B.S. in Chemistry and is a reiki master with Kamala Moon, LLC. She is currently training to become a massage therapist. She lives in southeastern Pennsylvania with her family and pets. In her free time, J.D. enjoys being active outdoors and is always up for new adventures. She also likes to paint and draw.

THE EMPATH EFFECT

Animals are the Best of Us
By Rebecca L. Wilson

Empath, and Veterinary Nurse

I heard the word empath in my late twenties, and I instantly knew I was one. Suddenly, I felt awakened in my desire to learn all about how to use this ability. In learning more, I realize there is a constant inner battle with my emotions getting the best of me. I have severe anxiety from feeling too much, especially in crowds of people. Within a few minutes of walking into a building or room, I can pick up on the general energy of everyone around me. I've been known to just up and leave places after this happens if I get an overall bad vibe from being there.

I am constantly trying not to feel every emotion. Sometimes, thoughts from other people come into my head. As you can imagine, it makes me insecure to hear what someone really thinks of me. It puts me in an awkward position of knowing too much about them way faster than anyone should. My relationships easily dwindle out if I feel deep down they are not a good person. I have this ability I call "the light switch," where I can strongly encourage someone to open up and tell me their life story.

When I was a bartender and customer service manager, this was a daily occurrence. When it happens, it always drains me, and I emotionally feel tied to that person until I can sleep and try to forget the connection. Sometimes they haunt my dreams, and I feel like I am that person, watching things play out with no ability to change the outcome of the story. The things that help me most are my animals. Petting them, matching my breathing with them, and lying beside them are my sources of mental healings.

Since I was a young child, I remember being scared of people; back then, I was called shy or antisocial. Now, as an adult, I understand it was because I felt too much and had no idea why I knew so many things about them. I used to think it was a really vivid imagination. I definitely could sense the evil in one of my relatives. I made sure to stay far away from him and hated when he was in the same house as me. At times, I had vivid dreams about what he had done before I understood what it was; and it terrified me to be around him.

There are so many other stories of feeling bad vibes, or what people may call auras around me, and not trusting those people. There was no definitive proof they were bad people, but I always just knew.

Human relationships can be incredibly complicated with the wide range of emotions you can feel from just one person; it's a weird thing to get a handle on as a kid. To cope with the overwhelming emotions from humans, when

I'd go somewhere, I'd find an animal and just be with it the rest of the party or event. They made my scary inner thoughts manageable and gave me courage in a way no person ever did.

Animals have always been so simple for me to hear, feel things the way they do, and connect to them without it being draining. They always bring me joy to be near them, though I never fully understood I had this gift to communicate with them. I always felt drawn somewhere when one was hurt.

I brought home many injured wild animals, much to my parent's dismay. A baby orphaned deer that needed to be brought to a wildlife rescue, baby birds whose nest was destroyed, a baby bunny who was bitten by a dog… the list goes on throughout my formative years.

Animals have helped me find a purpose in life and understand that I am a caretaker to the guardians that walk beside us.

My best friend was my shelter rescue dog, Tuffy, who I picked out as my early Christmas present when I was six. He was a border collie mix and the smartest dog I knew. I felt the happiest when he was asleep at my feet, protecting me. He was my true guardian, my angel on this plane, and I felt that instantly the day he came home with me. To this day, even with him crossed over so long ago, I can feel him watching over me at times.

Two decades after getting my first dog, I was aimlessly going through life without a true purpose, floating from job to job. I pursued a degree I felt no passion about, just to say I had one. Eventually, another mutt came into my life - a puppy named Frisbee who was black and white - the same colors as my childhood dog. He was in need of a home on an adoption website, and my fiancé and I wanted another dog to keep our first one company while we worked.

We knew he was the one the second we saw his face; his eyes looked pleadingly into ours, begging us to give him a happy life. We drove two hours to get him, and luckily, we were picked to take him home. After a few hours, diarrhea started pouring out of his tiny body. He was dying, and I felt it as he looked at me so helplessly. We looked up the closest emergency vet and rushed there in the early hours of what was turning into a terrifying morning.

Our worst fears were confirmed, and he was given a thirty percent chance of making it, even with very expensive medical intervention. We decided then and there - we were not giving up on our little man. We ended up using all of our honeymoon money to save his life. As he is my whole family's best friend and companion, currently still with us almost twelve years later, we will always tell you he was worth every penny we spent.

In learning about the parvovirus that almost took his life, I began to research other things as well. That ignited this fire and desire for more knowledge on how to take better care of my dogs. The desire spread, so I researched how to be a veterinary nurse and enrolled in a college to get my degree. It was good timing, as I had just come to the end of an era as a manager of one company that was closing permanently. I knew this was my chance to pursue something else and go in a new direction. I started feeling really excited about a career for honestly the first time in my working life.

Soon after, I began volunteering as a tech in a shelter. I loved it and learned so much in my time there. I also ended up with three cats and a third foster-fail dog who we fell in love with, which rounded out our pack. To date, we have fostered hundreds of dogs and over fifty cats.

We have slowed down a lot since having kids, so I try to volunteer, with what scarce free time I have these days, to always be involved in some role in rescuing animals. I'd love to run a rescue shelter as a medical director someday when my kids are a bit older. I want to educate the general public on the importance of not overpopulating the animal world, especially with ones passing on genetic problems.

Animals have helped me find a purpose in life and understand that I am a caretaker to the guardians that walk beside us.

They are our companions that help us through some of the loneliest and hardest times in our lives. The connection they have to the other side is much stronger than ours. Animals also have an undying loyalty that humans selfishly do not possess. When I feel an owner's deep connection in this way to their animal, I respect that power, and it is a beautiful thing to witness.

The flip side to that is not all of them get happy lives with loving owners. One such story sticks out in my mind because it was early on in my working career. A large golden retriever came into my hospital. The owner stated that he was an outside dog and had not eaten his food or moved much from his doghouse in a few days. This was happening in the middle of a very cold winter, and this dog was a senior.

As I was alone with the dog, I will never forget the clear feeling of a voice telling me his life story. He started out as a cared-for cute puppy that the owner got as a gift for his spouse. They were busy and worked a lot, and he chewed things up out of boredom, never knowing when they'd come home. He had an accident one day while waiting to be let out. They were both so mad one hit him with a rolled-up newspaper, and the other pushed his face into it.

He was shoved outside for hours until dark, where he cried to come back inside. He did his best never to have an accident again, but then the owners found a chewed-up shoe. His teeth were coming in, and it felt good to chomp on that leather. He was punished and thrown outside of the house. Then, he started shedding everywhere, and they had just gotten brand new furniture, so he was put outside again. For years this went on until they gave him a doghouse outside, and he never was allowed in anymore.

If there was a bad storm or snow, they'd open the garage and let him sleep on an old worn blanket. His only friends became the mice that visited him. He shared bits of food with them. This poor old boy was lonely and defeated; in that instant, I could feel the cold blackness he felt - all over my own body. He told me without words that he was leaving now, and he was done being a burden to his owners.

Feeling this, I cried my eyes out, holding him, petting him, and letting him feel every ounce of love I could send from inside me. He looked up into my eyes, saw my soul, and thanked me for caring. Then he took his last breath in my arms with a sigh of relief; the pain was finally over, and I felt his spirit leave his physical being and hover above us.

As I prepared his body, I sang sweetly to him and told him what a good boy he had been. None of it was his fault, and he did not deserve to be treated so unkindly while on this earth. When I was done, I felt him leave, and he felt at peace for the first time in a long time.

I carry this and many more stories with me, as do my colleagues. Being a great nurse, doctor, or support staff in the veterinary field is made difficult by many stressors, including convenience euthanasia (something none of us ever want to witness), behavior ones where we never get to know all the surrounding circumstances, or the animal abuse cases like my sad one here.

In our field, the absolute best of us are empaths, and it can be a burden to feel so much. I wish more people knew what we do. We are the doctors' eyes and ears, the lifesaving helpers, the comforters of your anxious pets, the ones who sing songs while we clean up after them all day and night. We carry around the stressed ones like swaddled babies to keep them calm while we continue doing a hundred other things seamlessly and never stop moving.

I hope my story helps other empaths in this field understand why we are so important and that we were chosen to take care of the voiceless for a reason. I hope you know I see all of you and consider you my sisters and brothers in our task of saving lives. If we ever cross paths, I will feel our kinship and help you on the worst days. I hope you see me too.

To all the empaths reading this part of the book, I hope you freely send love and light to all of us. My story is one of many, and we are all saving souls and helping heal our world together.

One wish I have is for all of us to feel peace with everything we are capable of and use our gifts to help ease each other's suffering, including our beloved animals. I think this is the biggest reason we were given this special ability by the creator. Thank you for reading my story, and I hope it inspires you to care more deeply for the wonderful creatures that live on this planet.

Rebecca L. Wilson, CVT has Business Management, and Veterinary Technology degrees. She has been a vet nurse for over a decade and has volunteered for rescues as a foster and held other leadership positions. Her most important role these days is being a mom to two amazing boys who just turned four and six and keep her busy. In her free time, she loves to read, hike in nature with friends, watch TV series (anything sci-fi), and have fun adventures with her husband, friends, and kids. Born and raised in Chester County, Pennsylvania, she is a country girl at heart.

Not Your Average Empath; Not Your Average Girl
By Kelly Krawczynski, MA, MFT

Trying to fit into a box has never been for me, and the same goes for being an empath. When I started to dip my toes into the spiritual world, I didn't know where I would fit in. However, like all lessons I've learned in life, it all seems to have a way of coming together in the end.

The main area I gravitated to was astrology; this is where my soul really started to get excited and awakened. I began where most people do, I learned about my sun sign, and as an Aquarius, I realized this is why I value authenticity and individuality, but I also have a deep concern for the collective and the well-being of all.

This helped me to understand how I can be myself and, at the same time, care for others. From here, I branched off to learn about intuition, empaths, and a whole host of other terms and phrases that came with opening the door to a world I had yet to explore. Even though these topics always interested me, we don't live in a society that offers this type of education; therefore, I was under the impression that if you didn't learn it when you were young, then it wasn't meant for you.

Obviously, I know now that this is false, but then the question becomes about "fitting in," which, as an Aquarius, can be hard to do. In fairness, it can be hard for anyone to do if being conventional isn't for you. When it came to labeling myself as an empath, I needed to define the term in a way that was right for me, even if it's not what others consider 'normal.'

To understand my journey, let me take you back to 2014. This is where my life really started to change to what it is now. It was a dark period for me. My relationship of ten years had just ended, and although I completed grad school, I was having trouble finding a job in the field I had spent so much of my life preparing for. I felt lost inside and had no idea what to do next.

I wanted answers but didn't know where to get them. Then one night at a street fair, I saw a small table with a sign for "Tarot Readings." This intrigued me; I found the mystical world fascinating, but this was the first time an opportunity to have a reading had ever presented itself. Here was my chance to try it out, and if it didn't work - then oh well, no harm done. I would just move on and continue searching.

To my delight, this would end up being one of the most pivotal moments of my transformation. The card reader was named Donna, ironically the same as my mother. She got a lot right, and she was caring, but it was a different kind of caring than I had seen from others in the past. She had a gift that allowed her to connect and empathize with me where she knew what I was experiencing without me saying a word. What gift allowed her to do that?

After that night, I was hooked. I looked for her at every street fair, and we got to know each other pretty well, or rather, she got to know me. I knew she was talented, but I didn't quite know how, so I started to expand my knowledge of this world. Of course, I continued to get readings because I still wanted answers. What I didn't understand was that I was asking the wrong questions. It wasn't about love or career; it was about something else. I did not know what question to ask, then one day, Donna gave me the right answer.

I don't remember what we were talking about or what the reading was about that day, but I remember she looked at me and said, "Well, you have the gift too, you know." From this point on, my new mission was to figure out what she meant.

This was where my mind and my universe really started to evolve. I became aware of what intuition was and how to tap into it. It was a process that took patience, but as I learned, was well worth it. At first, I had to learn that intuition is that little voice inside that tells you exactly what you need to know when you need to know it. It came in many forms; for me, it was mainly through my thoughts.

My intuition's communication is fast and persistent, it comes with an added urgency, and that's when I know I should listen. The feeling is hard to explain unless you let yourself experience it. I learned there is a name for this: clairvoyance. There are many types, but I was experiencing claircognizance, which is when you receive messages through your thoughts.

Next, I had to learn to trust my intuition; that was the hard part. As with any skill, it takes practice, and the more you use your intuition, the more comfortable you become with allowing it to guide you. Of course, to practice using my intuition, I had to start doing readings for others. At this point, I was still looking for a job as a counselor but had no luck, which meant I had plenty of time to do readings.

What I quickly realized was that blending therapeutic training and intuition made perfect sense. The best readings are when someone who cares taps into their intuition to confirm the messages your soul is trying to tell you. Just like I started going for readings when I was looking for help, I found others were too.

Although it might be considered "unconventional," it is the type of help and guidance that can offer reassurance in a way that traditionally can be hard to find in our world. When communicating an intuitive message, it takes being honest but compassionate, and authentic but helpful. Those are the same skills a counselor needs, except one must access their intuition, allowing it to lead the way.

I started to identify with the term intuitive, but empath? That was still a struggle. I understood the concept that certain people have the ability to feel what others are feeling without experiencing their pain firsthand, but I couldn't check all the boxes for being an empath. For one thing, I watch intense, suspenseful genres that most empaths don't enjoy.

At the time, two of my favorite shows were *The Walking Dead* and *Game of Thrones*, shows that some empaths would normally avoid because they would be overwhelmed with emotions. For me, it was different. I didn't get too anxious or scared; it was the opposite. I found myself getting excited and filled with adrenalin. I would want to be in the scene right by the side of the characters I had come to love and cherish.

The best way I can describe it is that my imagination would start to run wild, and instead of going to a dark place like some empaths do, I felt a need to connect to the world that I was exposed to through cinema. I was led to believe this was not a traditional response for an empath, but tradition isn't for everyone, and we all respond to our emotions differently. No two humans are alike, and neither are any two empaths.

Of course, television and movies weren't the only way I felt different from other empaths. In my research into this world, I discovered that the average empath cares so much

---

You will take that empathy and become a warrior. A warrior for those who are suffering, a warrior for those who are in pain, and a warrior for those who need to heal.

---

for others that being around those in pain can cause them to feel pain as well. I didn't connect to this either because I don't absorb my feelings for others; instead, it inspires me to help them.

I always wanted to go toward those in pain because I figured I could handle it, so it must mean I'm supposed to be near it. This is why I was drawn to helping professions. Being with those in need and providing compassion was something that came naturally. It's why I wanted to be a therapist and what I was looking for when I was lost and searching for answers.

I don't get bogged down with the emotions of others, which is a classic trait of empaths. Instead, I feel a need to do what I can to help as many as possible. There is, however, one exception, and that is with animals. Witnessing an animal in pain has always been emotionally triggering for me. It turns out I fit the classic definition for an empath when it comes to animals.

Throughout my journey towards self-discovery, I have had many realizations about myself and about the world we all live in. All of us have a gift to share that will undoubtedly help someone somewhere. We may not come to those gifts the way we think we would, but nevertheless, they are there for us to find.

I have come to define an empath by my own terms, even if it means I don't check all the boxes. Being an empath means you have increased empathy for humans, animals, and the earth. Sometimes it will make you sensitive, but other times, you will take that empathy and become a warrior. A warrior for those who are suffering, a warrior for those who are in pain, and a warrior for those who need to heal.

Kelly Krawczynski is the owner and practitioner of Pathways 2 Healing. She holds a master's degree in marriage and family therapy and is a certified intuitive counselor. Over the years, she has devoted many hours to studying astrology and has had the privilege of taking courses taught by some of the world's most renowned astrologers. She believes in the power of combining traditional therapy techniques with new age practices such as astrology and tarot to create a holistic approach to healing. To learn more about her services, like and follow her at www.facebook.com/Pathways2Healing, or to schedule a reading or session, email Kelly at pathways2healingservices@gmail.com.

All You Need Is Love: A Story of an Empath who Didn't Need Fixing
By Lijana Kikilasvili

Have you ever tried to fit in so hard that you ended up losing your identity?

When empaths absorb the energy of people around them, life becomes intolerable. They not only feel everything to the bone but also live it as if it were theirs. From a young age, I was fond of plunging into the void. I never truly felt any sense of belonging. People were 'strange,' yet I longed to make a myriad of friends and learned that being alone is not necessarily 'lonely.' To me, having a few dear ones is better than a legion of fakes.

I was scared to live yet refused to die. How ironic. My grandmother was of pure Lithuanian descent from the Upper Lands, the region known as Aukstaitija. My biological grandfather was indigenous to the Kartvelian people of the Kakheti region of Sakartvelo (Democratic Republic of Georgia). But I grew up with a grandfather from Southeast Lithuania.

I lived in a tiny apartment in an old-fashioned building on Immanuel Kant Street in Klaipeda city of Lithuanian Republic. I began school at six years old. Soon enough, I was called out as different and not a kid with whom peers would make friends. My last name stood out, and I had luscious black hair that touched my buttocks.

I was not the only kid in class who was practically an orphan. My peculiar origins (I am of Balt and Kartvelian descent) and the family story were reasons to get picked at, called at, pushed and shoved, etc. I experienced bullying every single day of my complicated childhood.

Our class had an art assignment to draw trees while looking out the window as a reference. "Your tree is crooked. Trees are not supposed to be crooked. Look out the window. Did you understand the assignment?!" This is what my teacher said to me. I complained to my grandmother (may she rest in peace); she had to step in and assertively protect her granddaughter. Trees can be dreadfully crooked (apparently).

During a yearly celebration of Mardi Gras, we had to make scary face masks. As I refused to make mine, our teacher got upset. She made the mask for me and went on saying, "You are too hard-headed and do not listen. So thus far, you will be named a goat for the Mardi Gras celebration.

Put this goat mask on!" I became a mocking goat of the week.

My native tongue teacher and I had a thing going. We could not stand each other. My hairclips did not please her. "What is that Lijana, are you a gypsy? What are those jingles in your hair?!" The whole class would explode in laughter. Some teachers rejected me since I was not Lithuanian enough.

I was a misfit. "What's wrong with me? Why can't I be like any other kid, like, normal? I coped by playing dumb for most of the curriculum, with the exception of the arts, sports, and biology classes. You know the story "boys will be boys," as I sat watching two boys roaming and arguing in the classroom, kicking chairs trying to hit one another, one hit my chair. "You shitty Georgian, get the hell out of here! Your black hair stinks!" Those words cut deeply. I was bullied at home the same way by the inner circle, neighbors, and their kids. I burst into tears. It never occurred to me to tell them that my mother is half Lithuanian and that I had every right to be there. But bygones are bygones now.

The school was terrifying, and I did not want to be their laughingstock again. Our local park was around twenty minutes by foot from home. It was raining 'cats and dogs,' but trees relaxed me, and all I did was daydream. I did not realize a drunken forty-year-old man was sitting by my side. "Excuse me, for how much are you selling yourself?" he asked. My head turned heavy, and I thought to myself, "Did I hear that right?" I cannot recall what I mumbled to him, but I ran away.

I came home feeling nauseous head to toe, and my guts were turning inside out. Granny made dumplings that day, I had no breakfast, and the whole kitchen smelled heavenly. "I am not hungry Granny, Roxette is on the radio." Music was another refuge out of a variety of tools that felt therapeutic to me. "Listen to your heart" was my favorite song. But what does that even mean? A twelve-year-old girl did not know the meaning of the song. All I could pronounce was "listen to your heart." That phrase was comforting and stuck with me for years.

My grandparents had been drinking for a few days and nights in a row. I didn't know which one was more unbearable the stench of alcohol, the cigarette buds all over the place, or the fact that I was starving. It was nighttime already, and I hadn't eaten yet.

In my bed, my head under the pillow, I covered myself from head to toe. "Okay, let's try to sleep now." I tried hard to fall asleep, but the noise from the other side of the room kept me awake for most of the night. The adults were arguing over something. The argument ended up in a gruesome fight. So I wept for my grandmother and prayed for her not to get beaten to death. I was terrified, I felt like throwing up, and my whole body ached. "Maybe, if I won't move, grandpa won't notice I am here?"

They were alcoholics, and any penny they had, they used it to buy spirits. We barely had food on the table. "Make sure you don't give her food. She has a mother; let her go there!" I went to bed hungry again. As usual, my granny saved some food for me. "When grandpa is asleep, go and eat it. It is all yours. Okay?" Later that night, she was beaten for it. Again.

It was snowing, and grandpa was out drinking, so I wandered into the stillness. I thought to myself, "What should we draw? Butterflies, we love butterflies." Then I got interrupted by grandpa. "Lijana, look what I have for you. You love these candies. Come and have a chat with grandpa." He was a complete mess and reeked of alcohol. I had to sit next to him to watch him drink to get my candies. Later that night, was it two or three o'clock in the morning, grandpa had put me outside in the snow. "You, go back to your mother. You are not eating my food. Step back inside, and I will kill you!" I stayed three hours at the entrance of our old building in my pajamas.

These early experiences of difficult life were all I knew back then. Much later, I've moved in with my aunt and uncle. They had two younger boys, my cousins. I did not feel accepted right away, and we needed time to get used to sharing space like a family. There was one incident that marked me for a long time. During breakfast, the boys were arguing over a missing teaspoon. The youngest one did not get his spoon, so he stole one from his brother. The table was accidentally shaken, and a cup full of boiling water fell on me. I burned my legs, and we rushed to a nearby hospital. One of our well-known doctors treated me like an animal. I thought I was living a nightmare.

I had a wonderful friend with whom I shared a special bond. We'd meet up as often as possible, and I had a few sleepovers at her place. I was two years older than her. The day before her birthday, she invited me to hang out. We drank beer, laughed a lot, and cooked some traditional food. In the morning, I found out that she hung herself. I lost my best friend to suicide on her birthday. Life was scary, people were appalling, and I hated myself for not being normal. I coped by indulging in sweets as often as I could to numb the sick feeling of my existence.

Body shaming was usual at home, and I could not look in the mirror. I had no pretty clothes, was ashamed of myself, my appearance, and my family. Often humiliated at school, I retreated to a corner to daydream.

My entire life, I listened to the guidelines thrown at me by others: you are too sensitive, you are too clean, too stupid, too rough, anxious, weird, useless, etc. It became the script of my reality. Being a loner and introvert were coping tools to protect my energy. I could not handle random noises and certain odors. Too easily distracted, constantly overthinking, overanalyzing, at the peak of the emotional roller-coaster, and crashing in angry outbursts. I cried a lot too.

Mood swings, déjà-vu, lucid dreams. Like a natural human lie detector, my inner knowing was heightened.

I saw through people's lies and their hidden agendas. Gatherings were too loud for me to handle, and I often retreated into a corner so I could breathe. During family dinners and special occasions by my aunt, you'd always find me under the table chowing down smoked sausage with ketchup and bread. I wanted to be left alone and was always hungry. Physical and emotional shutdowns were my everyday normal.

Another issue was difficulty sleeping because my mind felt overstimulated. Energy is information that your whole system needs to process. We receive this information from countless sources twenty-four/seven. Empaths tend to sponge that in and quite often store it in their bodies. Tired during the day, I had too many ideas at night. The only way to get it out of my system was to write or sketch on countless pieces of paper. That is how I accumulated tons of notepads, notebooks, sketchbooks, and post-its.

Empaths draw in other people's feelings, pain, stress, and toxic energy from places, items, non-physical beings, and more. We live with anxiety, depression, fibromyalgia, or other auto-immune disorders, and burnout. We don't do well under drugs, anesthesia, and alcohol. Food sensitivities and deficiencies are common. Our diets need to be as clean as possible. But seeing how we don't understand what is happening to us, we numb our senses with toxic food, alcohol, sugar, drugs, etc.

The worst place to work, for an unaware empath, is a nursing home, hospital, angry office, school, etc. Via our empathic abilities, we can naturally tune in with people at their level. The service we deliver is one hundred times more than expected of us. Because we are incognizant of these abilities, we end up suffering somatic ailments. Empathy and high sensitivity are not disorders. One of the worst phrases that an empath can hear is, "It's all in your head!"

What others don't know is that our bodies vibrate at a very high frequency. Our system naturally transmutes whatever we take in. However, we don't always release it, and it gets stored in our organs, endocrine, and an immune system like the lymphatic system, for example. Inflammation is common to experience for empaths. That's why the choice of food we ingest is crucial for our physical and mental health. Breathwork is beneficial to balance the fire energy in our bodies.

I heard that empathy is considered a weakness. I used to hide my feelings and emotions. Put on a poker face as a mask when faced with certain situations and cry a river behind closed doors. People would often say to me, "Don't be too happy, don't be too sad, too shy, too open, too closed off, be diplomatic, not too thick-skinned, don't speak your mind, you look angry, you are too intolerant, you don't have to be so sensitive."

People like us are natural healers. We crave healing while out there trying to heal others. Most of us are people-pleasers too. Triggered by trauma that we are unable to process, our senses get extra heightened in these moments. We have difficulty internalizing our emotions. We don't live well the exclusion part, the rejection, and have difficulty accepting the division or separation between races, classes, and the natural world. Ask every empath out there, and they will affirm that: we are all one!

In 2007, I was diagnosed with depression. I had episodes of anxiety and panic attacks every day. I experienced these episodes while walking on the street, taking a shower, having lunch, or while sleeping. At a certain point in my life, I nearly lost it, trying to take pills with alcohol so that tomorrow never came. There was no point in living.

In 2010 the path began to shift, and in 2012 was the last time I experienced a panic attack. Fast forward three years, I came across the terms empath and highly sensitive. It shook my world, and the foundations began to crumble. The old paradigm on which I built myself, and my life, did not make sense. It was such an eye-opener. I started to understand why I had issues with crowded places, dentists, hospitals, planes, busses, schools, etc.

Empaths need to learn healthy boundaries. We need to decompress daily and make sure we go out in nature as much as possible. So, what are the tools that I used to initiate the healing process?

There is nothing to fix. I am not broken but cracked open for the healing to take place.

Every night I went to bed with a recorded hypnosis session. Then I incorporated morning meditation and automatic writing daily. I practiced self-forgiveness, self-acceptance, and self-validation (vs. external validation) of every emotion I felt. Whenever I noticed patterns in my reaction to life, people, places, and situations, I gave myself as much time as needed to get to the root of the cause.

For example: Why did I try to please people so much? Was I trying to accomplish good deeds? Maybe I needed external approval that I was good enough? Or maybe seeing others suffer made me suffer, too, so I rushed in and offered help. I could not understand why the unsolicited help was rarely appreciated.

My lesson was to learn to observe and not absorb. To allow others to explore their path. Another example - I gave too much of myself. Be it advice, a smile, a shoulder to cry on, a penny, or whatever. Why did I feel so empty and drained? Did I want something in return? Why did I feel uncomfortable receiving compliments, gifts, and help from others? Why did I put myself last?

Do you see a pattern of self-sacrifice here? Self-worth issues as a result of tough childhood were the truth I needed to face and learn to accept it as-is. Inner work was what I did to liberate myself from what did not belong to me, what was a projection from broken caregivers, school systems, peers, and so on.

Is there a happy ending?

Fast forward another six years, I love and accept myself as I am. I watch what I put into my body. I don't look down on and don't speak ill of myself. I learned that what we see, hear, and ingest - we become. I don't need to prove my worth to the world or convince everyone to like me. There is nothing to fix. I am not broken but cracked open for the healing to take place.

Today, I embrace every part of myself that made me who I am. I am perfectly imperfect. I am a hundred percent authentic me. Life still gets tough, and now and then, I happen to take that roller-coaster ride. Be it a few unhealthy snacks or not wanting to socialize, I am still profoundly in love with the way I am.

The truth is, there is no need to apologize or explain to anyone how and what I do or don't do. Empathy is my gift to the world. It has helped me re-discover my innate abilities, which led me to develop my practice to help others like me. The dark is not scary; it's nurturing. We are like seeds that take time to grow when buried in the ground.

So dear empath, whether you are a nurse, a doctor, a teacher, a mental health practitioner, or a prison officer: surround yourself with loving people, cut out everything that does not support your well-being, and love yourself first. We need you in these fields of expertise.

Treat people as a whole, i.e., body, mind, and spirit. Holistic medicine is one of the tools that can help you and others in finding recovery and comfort when you come home to your families from an intense and often dense workplace. Empaths need healing from being physically and emotionally drained. As we all deserve to live healthy lives that lead to happiness.

If health is not our wealth, then what is?

Lijana Kikilasvili is a shamanic facilitator, universal healer, spirit channel, and scribe. With over six years of experience in holistic/alternative medicine, she specializes in emotional, trauma, and pain release. She facilitates inner healing through a soul-embracing journey. Lijana studied with Dr. Steve G. Jones (Ph.D.) and Cyndi Dale (internationally bestselling author, intuitive, healer). She is a certified neuro-linguistic programming (NLP) practitioner and a spiritual life coach. Fun fact about her: Lijana is indigenous to the Balts and Kartvelians. Find her at divinesoulspark.com. She would be delighted to connect with you.

Awakening
By Sarah J. Faaborg

The journey toward enlightenment and my awareness of being an empath began as far back as my memory allows. I was not aware of my differences as a child and would face many challenges and obstacles over the years. Looking back, I now understand the awakening of my uniqueness and this beautiful gift.

The memories I have are unusual because I was of such a young age, an infant and toddler.

As a toddler, I remember sensing feelings, the patterns on outfits, and even the emotional reactions of both myself and those around me. Even feelings from birth, like a dream. I grew to appreciate this unique difference from others, but it was not that way in the beginning.

I was named after my great-grandmother, and the stories I was told of her remind me of my inner discovery of self. I never did get to meet my great-grandmother, as she passed away years before I was born. I feel close to her in spiritual ways and honored to carry our name Sarah and perhaps some other traits of uniqueness we shared.

Looking back into my childhood, I was very blessed to spend time in a small northern California coastal town off Highway 1, bordering the Sonoma and Mendocino County lines. The Gualala River mouth opened to the Pacific Ocean as my front yard, and the redwood forest was my back yard. I explored the open countryside and roamed with our family dog, a German Shepherd named Bear, always at my side. I was the youngest at the time, living with my parents and two older brothers.

My age was young, but my soul felt old and intuitive, as if I had already lived hundreds of years. I never skipped a beat connecting with others and sensing their feelings before words were spoken. I sensed pain and unspoken heaviness and tried to adjust myself to comfort others. Having that keen sense of human need and understanding, adjusting my sensitive sensory systems, intuitive sense, and dream-like déjà vu feelings would become my strengths and weaknesses.

Full of happiness, naturally, I learned that it would be others' reactions to my ways that would damage my sense of self-confidence. I realized I could work on this weakness with practice, balance, purpose, intentions, and humbled self-understanding. I would learn how to shed others' opinions of myself and find my way.

AWAKENING

We are born innocent and then groomed by systems, surroundings, and choices; without guidance, we can be re-programmed and influenced by negativity in life. When I turned forty and reflected back on my childhood, I understood how the awakening happened.

I was probably just five or six years old, taking what seemed like a long walk down the berm of grass to enjoy the view from my coastal home. Secluded by trees and large rocks, I would sit and look at the massive Pacific Ocean and smell the crisp salted air, hear the crashing of the distant waves and underlying roar of the ocean, and see the far-off horizon. In the distance, I could glimpse the passing of a barge or the spray from a whale.

Sometimes I would lay and stare at the seagulls flying above, listening to the sounds the swallows made nesting, the crows talking, and the finches singing nearby. I became aware of the different birds, their sounds, shapes, and colors and wondered what gave them the ability to fly and look and sound different.

While sitting very still, I would watch the flowers bloom, amazed by each blossom and color, opening so delicately as each petal unfolded and straightened in its softness, the bees pollinating yet remaining cautious.

Often, I would sing to the flowers or the animals and think to myself, "What amazingness surrounds me and surely how magical this all is." Before I even understood the world's teachings of religions, I would ask myself, "What made these things? Who gave me the ability to feel so much?" I had conversations with what I would later come to believe is God, that higher power of energy, the creator. I would ask myself, "What made me, and why do I seem different from others?"

I would see the family dog watch me watching nature, observing his response as if in that very moment we were comparing notes. I had conversations in my mind with the dog, feeling the dog communicate without words. I found that animals are the gentlest, for they are not like humans and have no need for opinions and judgments. I would feel other energy frequencies and sometimes scary feelings I did not understand in shadows and dark places.

While exploring, I would run as fast as I could, staring up to the redwood trees soaring tall above, and could feel the years of growth while hearing the moaning trees swaying in the wind. I experienced intuitive feelings from all of life's creations.

I grasped the immense cosmic energy all around us and in me as well. This was my awakening to the creator and to my abilities. The ability to feel more than I see, to communicate with more than what most hear, and to react versus simply feel. I became even more intuitive when I trusted in the signs coming from within me.

This was not just becoming aware and conscious; it was an awakening of the spiritual being inside me. Over time I learned that my gifts as an empath are awareness and self-acceptance. I spent most of my life questioning it. Looking back, I wish I had learned that being different was not bad or wrong and how other people viewed or reacted to me didn't matter.

My brain saw patterns; I felt energy everywhere, including with humans and other creations. I was different and processed things differently. Naturally, I manifested happiness from the heart, not the brain.

Perhaps differences in the brain and heart stimulate responses that make balance hard to sustain. I would learn to manifest positive patterns of happiness from the heart as I did naturally as a child, stripped of the world's toxic opinions of differences. I realized I allowed the world to suppress me. This balance between the chaos of energy I felt from other life and natural intuitive visions and feelings was so important to understand. I needed to control my responses and discipline my reactions.

I wanted to improve my responses and reactions when I shared my gift with others. Many times, I made bad choices based on sensitive feelings with behavior vs. intuitive instinctive responses. I fell subject to believing others, becoming clogged with opinions. This experience actually helped me to evolve into a better version of self. Some would say I was learning the hard way. I reflected and noticed when I was thinking too hard to respond versus intuitively responding, knowing myself best.

Mastering the way of connecting with creation, I was flexible in communicating because the flow of the patterns can change. Not all creations speak as humans do. When we are in our empathetic and sensitive selves, we tap into our energy, feel what is coming from within us, what is coming from around us, and can translate various energies into what other humans can understand.

Understanding nature's way with humans, each experience gives us practice, conditioning us to become better at it. Perhaps some are born with stronger sensors than others, but this doesn't mean that the ability to communicate empathically cannot be learned in one's life through constant practice and conditioning.

As I grew to grade school age, so often I would hear, "You're too sensitive." "You are so direct." "You think you know everything." "You are intimidating." "Why are you always so happy?" or "You are so weird." These sorts of comments caused me to judge myself and become insecure and sensitive causing years of self-sabotage. This made me feel as if I needed to cater to what other people wanted, never feeling accepted for who I was.

I went through a period of several years questioning who I was, second-guessing my own self-confidence and feelings of the heart. I practiced meditation and prayer, searched for answers to change the hurtful patterns bombarding me from all directions. I couldn't change anyone else, but I could refine my own way.

I knew I was not how others described me. I learned that acting differently to satisfy others still did not please the very people who, in fact, were themselves behaving what they preached was the problem in me. Most never saw my pain. They saw it too late when the pain turned to anger and concluded that it was me who had a problem.

Feeling sensitive inside, I would cry and ask myself, "Am I normal? What is normal? Do I have control? God only knows what I hold back and keep to myself." I knew the people around me would never understand until they reached that level of awareness and consciousness within themselves. They didn't know what they were showing through actions. They were living in denial. Those who fight the nature of an empath may not be ready for the truth. They may not be ready to confront themselves with their own ways and their own demons. An empath can see and feel them for who they truly are.

Other people didn't want to believe when I spoke of these differences or explained intuitive sensitivities. They didn't want to admit when I was right. It was easy to be taken as the bad person when I cared so much; some would say, too much. My intentions were innocent. I thought other humans should be able to do what I could do. It caused a great deal of anger, and I thought that others were not sensitive enough. We all have different timelines for when the self-enlightenment or acceptance of self becomes understood.

Perhaps some will never learn. I've seen people on their deathbeds who never learned. I've held many hands of people who passed on to the next part of their journeys, leaving this life behind. I've witnessed those in fear and questioning their lives when it was too late to make changes. While others may become enlightened at a young age. There are some who grow and learn throughout their entire life journey.

To understand the limitations and boundaries of being an empath, while striving to refine myself into the best version of "me," I took the path of public service in helping others, always knowing I could impact those in need. I worked in many roles with the opportunity to connect with people. I worked in demanding environments like emergency medical services and hospitals.

I went back to school to learn the specialty of electricity of the brain. Electrophysiology of the body was familiar to me, both self-experienced, sensing these patterns from a young age, then educationally applied. It was a full circle for me, coming back home to the very patterns that created the abilities within me, now with an understanding of the anatomy and physiology of the body and metabolic systems.

I learned how the body generates and conducts energy and patterns to sustain life, and it made sense to me. I witnessed, experienced, and encountered some of the best and worst situations one could ever imagine. Overstimulation effect? Or was the effect of the awakening?

Years later, randomly, I met a woman who asked if I was an empath. "What is an empath?" I asked. "Is that a bad thing or a good thing?" The explanation this amazing woman offered confirmed my feelings since childhood. It was as if she took a copy from within me to understand the individual imprint of my experiences and hard feelings of pain over the years. She is an empath; she felt and understood me.

*I learned to create boundaries between myself
and others and not allow them to shift my
feelings of self-understanding.*

Perhaps I still, from time to time, question if I am an empath or just ordinary. I question why others can't become more sensitive and adapt to being intuitive to other human's needs. There is much we don't understand about each other because there are so many different levels of sensitivity and uniqueness.

We must accept and understand the complexity of our brain, its functions, and its integrated process with our heart. We can use our sensory systems to improve the way we connect and communicate with the people around us. We can service others better by using our natural abilities and choosing a different response.

I came to realize that in my presence if someone had traits they didn't like, I would experience myself reflecting to them the truth they deny seeing in themselves. I had to be careful with this experience and monitor my responses. I held the mirror for others to see themselves. I learned how to differentiate the chaos coming from within self and that which came from outside of self. I learned how to balance and control the emotions and responses of others. That became the greatest exercise of my life, repeated regularly every day.

It was a grounding process that brought me back to the present and the reality of the moment. As humans, there is much happening between the brain and the heart. Behavior and reaction, brainwashed by external influence. Slow down and breathe, feel the moment, decipher where the energy is coming from, where the best focus can be found next to prayer and meditation. I would use these tools in my survival and self-care for my entire life.

I realized daily the positive influence I had on my surroundings. The positive returns would fill and strengthen me. It was a cycle. I am a woman who has endured experiences not wished upon anyone. However, the growth from these experiences is non-exchangeable in life. I have traveled and immersed myself in diversity, different cultures, and happiness.

One should be okay with losing and finding oneself, re-learning what love means, and having purpose and best intentions in this life. I invite you to look for your inner child, reflecting on your total experience and growth. The awakening journey is ongoing. Awareness and consciousness are a start. Don't be afraid to dive into yourself; embrace becoming comfortable with your deeper feelings.

I was forty-one years old when I learned the word "empath." Together, empaths share their ways and help others expand their self-awareness. For most empaths, they are an easy and sensitive target until they accept their gift with confidence.

The evolution of becoming aware of oneself is such an immense journey; our efforts show in our actions and our connections with each other.

It is difficult to carry oneself without outwardly showing emotional energy. Life has shown me that other humans cannot read me well, causing a mistake in the interpretation of many situations. I learned to create boundaries between myself and others and not allow them to shift my feelings of self-understanding. After all, we don't ask others how we feel. We must know ourselves best and then support the best version of "self."

I avoid trying to please others and guide them instead. Never forget to mold yourself first! Empaths already see and feel this happening, and they patiently wait while hoping the other person will begin an awakening process. It is delicate and possible. I practiced restraint in outward response and emotion, leaving those to the heart. I focused on hope, faith, and love.

I learned how to touch millions by guiding some to be more sensitive, at times more grounded, conscious, and aware of self and others. Empaths should reflect and embrace this uniqueness in self. There is much to see and feel when you slow down to embrace the uniqueness in you.

It is possible one can achieve a process of spiritual alchemy that works best for them as I did. Start by finding the inner peace in you no matter the differences and begin the awakening of oneself.

Sarah J. Faaborg is an Electroneurodiagnostic Technologist who has spent twenty-seven years in emergency medicine and healthcare. She is a writer, an optimistic visionist, a divine spiritual alchemist, an empath with a highly sensitive personality and sensory system, and a believer of God. Well-practiced in prayer, meditation, self-healing reiki, and following Sunnah medicine.

Her career path includes firefighter, emergency medical technician, EKG, and EEG Technician. Experienced in dealing with a complexity of behaviors and personalities. Associate Science degree in firefighting and a portfolio of certificates. A survivor of chronic pain, post-traumatic stress, and depression. Loves time with her children and parents. Loves to travel and has special love for Morocco.

Narcissist Meet Empath:
A Story of Growth
By Michelle Burd

You might see the title and think to yourself, "Ah. Yet another stereotypical story about an empath falling in love with a narcissist." You more than likely are right, or you might see the true beauty in the story and take it as a sign of strength and hope for all empaths currently stuck in this situation. Empaths attract narcissists, bottom line. They, the empaths, will try to change the narcissists and try to manipulate the situation by thinking it is a healthy and loving relationship. The empath normally finds strength after being broken down in every single sense of the word.

My story is one of growth, resilience, strength, and, more importantly, self-love.

I grew up in a broken home and with a load of childhood trauma ranging from witnessing the effects of substance abuse to being sexually molested for several years. These life experiences helped me grow, and I give them gratitude. They also showed me from a young age that I'm a feeler. I can feel everyone around me, and I am sensitive to the world around me.

Imagine being eight years old and holding your father as he cries in your arms. Taking his emotions and your emotions as you process the fact that you're holding your father as he is crying, and now add in feeling your own father's sadness and fear.

I knew from a young age, even before that monumental moment, that I was an empath. I cried at everything: people picking flowers because the flowers had feelings, trees being cut down to build new structures and roadways, and simply seeing other people cry. Being an empath is a gift and should not be tucked away or taken advantage of, and narcissists know how to take advantage of empaths.

The summer before my freshman year of college, I met my narcissist. The fun part about my story is that he was open and honest with me about being a clinically diagnosed narcissist. Did I see these red flags? Of course not! I don't even know what that means, but whatever it is, I can change him!

Almost six and a half years later, I am sitting here writing this story about how I could not change him, but I could step into my power and recognize my worth enough to remove myself from the situation. Narcissists like to love bomb and go way too hard, way too fast, and empaths will eat that up like we are children who hit the candy jackpot in our Trick-or-Treat bags (for me, it's the Butterfingers).

*It's taking back your freedom and establishing
a new sense of self-love that nobody can
penetrate because you, my dear empath, you
are worthy and perfect just the way you are.*

I could write an entire book on the warning signs and the experiences I went through, but it is important to know that no matter how bad it gets, you are worthy, and you can leave. I will share snippets of my story to show the highs and lows but also to prove that it does get better, and you will be free.

I was abused in every sense of the word. I came out of that relationship with so much more strength because I was free to be myself, and I found who I was truly destined to be.

As any relationship with a narcissist goes, there are highs, lows, and it can drastically switch from one end of the spectrum to the other end in a matter of seconds. Being in a relationship with a diagnosed narcissist meant justifying behaviors such as being screamed at for forgetting to buy the right brand of pasta sauce or not wanting to do the dishes because it was a long day at work. One time, I was screamed at and made to feel so small because I had decided to clean at an hour that was not feasible for his schedule.

He would play video games with his friends, and I would be left to clean up after him. I was constantly throwing away his trash because he would just let it sit there and expect me to do something about it. Then when I would do something about it, he would yell at me for doing something about it. This was the relationship for six and a half years.

When I would stand up for myself, he would berate me and tell me how he was there for me when my father died and how he was financially supporting me, and I couldn't live without him. These moments occurred far more often than I care to admit. As an empath, I took on his rage and felt it as disappointment, so I strived to do better. It takes so much strength and self-love to break this cycle, but when it finally is broken, it's so freeing.

One thing to note with narcissists is their ability to make a scene about a minor inconvenience you have caused them. My relationship was so controlled that I worked at the same place in the same area as him. When I took a new job making more money and given more freedom with scheduling, he wanted to do nothing more than control me.

My actions became his problem, and he was determined to change this.

As a result of this controlling behavior, he decided he would try to incite pity from me in hopes of changing my mind. He cried and put on a show hoping I wouldn't take the offer, and when that didn't work, the real narcissistic, manipulative behaviors began. He took a steak knife, left in his car, and didn't come back for hours. I knew that if I played along, he would have won, so I stayed silent and didn't call or text.

I think I watched a movie, to be honest with you. He came home to tell me his plan. He was planning to slit his throat and drive into a pole just to end it because life was getting too hard. This is the epitome of narcissistic behavior, and I did not play into it, which led to more and more attempts at manipulations. At this point, I was noticing these behaviors and taking my power back. He was fighting for any chance to manipulate me again, and I did not play into it.

I took my power back, and that was only the beginning of discovering my self-worth and my own freedom. I learned how great that feeling was, and I needed to feel it again and again.

When I finally decided it was time to leave, he punched a wall, broke his hand, and called me all sorts of names. I had just gotten out of the shower and felt like I needed to do it in that moment, or I would never be able to leave. I broke up with him completely naked, with my hair dripping wet.

It took me several hours to get him out of my apartment, and when I did, I could do nothing but cry. I was finally free. I collapsed on the bathroom floor and uncontrollably cried. I FaceTimed my mom, and all I could do was continuously spit out, "I'm free." At last, I was able to see and love myself enough to know I deserved to be treated well. The feelings of loving myself and taking my power back are the absolute best feelings in the world.

Discovering your worth and learning to love yourself again after recognizing and making the decision to no longer be with a narcissist is a wonderful feeling. It's hysterically crying on your bathroom floor, completely naked and wrapped in a towel while FaceTiming your mom and repeatedly saying, "I'm free." It's laughing to yourself as you help pack his car because he shattered his hand when he decided to punch the wall and blame it on you. It's taking back your freedom and establishing a new sense of self-love that nobody can penetrate because you, my dear empath, you are worthy and perfect just the way you are.

Hi! I'm Michelle. I began my spiritual journey in 2017 when my dad died of stage four glioblastoma (a rare and aggressive form of brain cancer). I grew up in a conservative Christian church that I wholeheartedly wanted to believe in, but there was always something there that did not make sense or something that I needed to question. When my dad passed, I learned the lesson of love. Everything is love. Through my awakening, I discovered what the heck an empath is and that I am one. This awakening led me to where I am today as you are reading this biography.

An Abrupt Awakening
By Rev. Matthew F. Thomas, AO.
ULC. SGC, RMT

To understand what it is to be empathic, one must understand how the world seems to an empath.

For me, it is disorderly, chaotic, unbalanced, and loud. For instance, try holding a conversation with someone at a heavy metal concert. Yeah, it's irritating and completely exhausting. This is why many, if not all, empaths seem to be ambiverts or introverts who love everyone but desperately need a lot of alone time to recover from social interaction. Heightened empathy is a miraculous gift but one that comes with very difficult challenges.

The word empathy is defined as a level of sympathetic understanding: cognitive, emotional, and compassionate. Having empathy means one can imagine themselves in another's situation and sympathize and understand what they might be feeling.

However, when speaking of being an empath, the word describes a person's emotional sensory level. Each individual empath has their own level of sensitivity, feeling vibratory frequencies of varying degrees. To explain further, let me try to paint a picture.

This world of ours is amazing and beautiful; however, it's cluttered with approximately seven billion living human beings, all with emotions coming at you simultaneously every day through a plethora of varied sensory input. To continue with our heavy metal concert metaphor, if the average person's volume runs from, let's say, 1-10, then the empath's factory default setting is 300. Are you starting to get the picture?

Imagine if you could remember vividly the moment you were born. What would that feel like? You're warm and comfortable, calm and serene until you begin to feel pressure closing in around you. A sensation of falling overcomes you, and you struggle to be free of your confines. Unable to determine which way is up or down, you writhe in an anxious panic until the pressure has stopped. Emerging into a vastness that chills your body, you are disoriented and confused, wailing in fear, flailing like a fish out of water, every nerve lit up like a Christmas tree until at last, you are wrapped in a blanket and set in your mother's embrace to warm you again.

This is how I remember my own birth. The first corporeal experience that I believe set my 'comfort level' from my first moments in this world. Every day after was, and still is, a struggle to sustain a status quo of comfort with my surroundings.

My mother's comforting arms became my definition of calm. The center of where I felt safe, and to this day, fifty-three years later, it is still my foundation. Building on that connection, I found similar calm with girlfriends and, eventually now for the last thirty years, in my wife's arms. The loving embrace of the women in my life and their hands that hold me with unconditional love anchors my world. Without that focal point, I don't dare imagine how lost I might be.

My memory of early childhood is a broken assortment of experiences that held emotional prominence. I say broken because, at age twelve, a personal tragedy shook my world and ultimately set me on my path in life. However, for the moment, let's set the stage.

My mother was a career nurse. In fact, as of the writing of this article, my mother (seventy-eight years old) is still working as a nursing supervisor at the same hospital she graduated nursing school from fifty-eight years ago. She is a woman of immeasurable strength and compassion.

My father was a city police lieutenant. Yes, the cliche pairing of a nurse and cop is quite common as they both worked in a life of service. My parents strived to never bring work home with them; it was the nature of these two souls, their dedication and courage, that set the tone of our home and family.

In addition to my parents, I think it's quite relevant to mention another prominent soul in my infancy, our springer spaniel, whose name was Heidi. When I was born, Heidi had just had a litter of pups, and being in maternal mode, she adopted me as well. I learned to stand and walk by holding on to her collar.

Heidi had a sixth sense when it came to me. Children may cry for many reasons, but Heidi was the kid whisperer. My parents only had to look at Heidi when I cried to know "why" I was crying. If the dog didn't move, I was fine. If the dog jumped up to see what was the matter, then it was something important.

The unconditional, unwavering love and loyalty of a dog and Heidi's affection for me contributed to my early empathic ability. Perhaps training me in a symbiotic way to sense another's emotional state. I did spend a lot of time with Heidi. Later in life, I still have a closeness with some animals. A Familiar, as witches like to call them.

I don't have an instant rapport with all animals. For instance, even from Heidi's pups, we kept one we named Missi. I didn't have the same connection to Missi as I had with Heidi. Throughout life, our family had many animals, but only the rare few did I connect with emotionally. As if they knew they were supposed to be my partner at that point in my life.

Currently, I have a golden doodle named Maggie. She heals me emotionally with a cuddle whenever I come home from work at the emergency room. She helps me release the emotions of the day and all the people I came in contact with, restoring me to my status quo state of inner peace.

Returning now to my childhood. I am four years older than my brother, and I'd like to say I had a closeness with him. We do share an unspoken loyalty as siblings, and to this day, we will always come to the other's aid without hesitation. But my path has always been a lonely one, sometimes by choice, sometimes by nature.

It matters not what the world is doing, but what you are doing in the world.

Our age difference also played a small part in our separation and my own difficulty associating with peers. Most of the children in our suburban neighborhood were either significantly older than me or just a bit younger. I did become popular for a short time as I aged into driving and being able to buy beer before anyone else, but otherwise, I kept to myself most of the time.

When my brother was born, we more or less lived separate lives in our family home, occasionally playing together, but I must confess I was often cruel to him. Perhaps out of jealousy as he was the baby. I don't really know why I tormented him as I did, and I now regret every instance of doing so; he didn't deserve any of it.

I say we lived separate lives because I was introverted and closed most of the time. I was enthusiastic and extroverted with my elders, conversing openly with any adult who would care to chat. This worried my mother a bit, whenever I would start chatting with complete strangers. My trust in my elders was unconditional and perhaps extremely naive. I still find more peace in the presence of my elders than my peers. Why? I have no idea.

Thus far, I have introduced my immediate environment and family in an attempt to explain my place within the world. I was a part of the family, but also very much just a tenant of the house, not especially connected in a conventional way. I always felt like I didn't quite belong.

Earlier, I spoke about a tragic event that eventually became the catalyst that shaped my life path. This was my abrupt awakening. I want this relating of my empathic journey to be instructive and not a fearful omen to anyone else looking for comfort as they are discovering their own coping means with their empathic ability.

As a boy, my relationship with my father was relatively textbook to the era of the 1970s. However, I was quite a curious nut to crack so far as creating a meaningful rapport. I was flighty, ever dreaming, and in some instances so deeply pensive that I was openly considered odd and possibly disturbed.

My father never gave up on me. He was a good father, as warm and loving as a stern street-savvy cop could be. He was the foundation of my world. He was my male role model, whom I was just beginning to understand by the age of twelve. Until the night it happened.

I could always feel everyone's general emotional state at any given time, and according to my extra-sensory perception, today was going to be bad. The day's activities were like any other with the daily routine of household puttering and random this and that, but I knew something was very wrong. That day felt strange.

The rattling sounds of activity in the house fell into the background as a sensation began to grow stronger and stronger. It was a heavy feeling, a numb feeling that captured the attention of all of my senses, urging me to search for what was causing it. Wandering the house, I felt my anxiety grow as the feeling intensified. I became distraught and panicked.

As I raced through the house following the heavy feeling, I came upon my father putting on his uniform getting ready to go to work. I had seen him get ready for work thousands of times before, but the heaviness was most pronounced around him.

His own mood was calm and content, but this feeling of heaviness surrounded him. Something was off. Something was wrong about dad, and whatever he was doing, he needed to stop. With what I was feeling, I concluded he should stop getting ready. He should not go out. We needed to remain all-together at home until whatever was causing this feeling went away.

At this point, I was hysterically crying and pleading, which came as a shocking surprise because though I was known to be exceedingly emotional, this was a hundred times worse than normal. I was terrified.

I was told to calm down and was handed off to my mother to deal with as my father continued to ready himself so he wouldn't be late. I remained inconsolable as he walked out the door.

Though I did calm down a little after he left, probably because the heaviness left with him, I was still uneasy and afraid. Night came, and I couldn't sleep. In fact, I came to learn that no one in the house seemed to be able to sleep. Roughly around 2 am, the phone rang.

My mother answered, and I ran to her closed bedroom door to find out who was calling. I could hear her talking. Then there was a sudden silence, and my mother began to cry. She hung up with the caller and quickly called her good friend and neighbor. In a sobbing outburst, she exclaimed, "Oh Terry, Edward is dead!"

The whole day prior, everything I was feeling was the first instance in my life when I had felt the approach of and the presence of death. I felt it, but no one else could, and I couldn't convince anyone else that something was very wrong. I spent the next nine years of my life torturing myself for not trying harder to keep him home. Also, in the subsequent nine years, I had to find the strength to find my center and regain my inner peace and status quo.

I shared this because it was a powerful story from my own life and to help anyone reading this understand how an empath feels things much more acutely than the average person. So much so that some empaths can sometimes even sense the approach of death.

I have felt the approach of death numerous times since, but the first time was soul rocking. Being that close to the threshold of what comes after our journeys from this life into the next truly changes one's perspective of what's important and reminds us to enjoy every moment we have together.

On the other hand, it also may make the things we busy our lives with, our dreams and aspirations, more or less trivial compared to what we know from these experiences. This is why empaths may find it difficult to get excited about things or even have the inspiration to mingle among our own species at all.

Here are my top six upsides to being an empath:

1 It's very hard, if even possible, to lie to an empath.

2 An empath's capacity for compassion is immense, which makes them fantastic healers and teachers.

3 Once an empath grows to be able (to some extent) to control their ability, they can positively transform energy with just their presence.

4 Empaths can find joy and light in the darkest places.

5 Empaths are vastly creative.

6 An empath's ability to love is immeasurable.

Each of us is sensitive to differing degrees and will experience the ability differently. Everything in this physical existence has a pro and a con, an upside and a downside.

I pray that my experience proves that no matter how uncomfortable your life may feel now or how dark the world may seem sometimes, I guarantee you that the sun will rise with every tomorrow. Greet every dawn with hope and thanks to our creator for who you are. You are special and an important part of this world.

Lastly, I want to share a few sayings that have helped me along the way. The first is, "Be in the world, not of it." (From *The 21 lessons of Merlin* by Douglas Monroe.) To me, this means empaths are here to help the people of this world feel more, which will aid them on their journey of self-understanding. If we allow ourselves to assimilate too completely into the "shared reality," we may lose ourselves in it.

The second saying is, "A thing isn't a thing until it becomes a thing. Until some thing happens and becomes a thing then there is no thing to worry about." (Rev. Matthew Thomas.) This one's mine, and it means to try your best to take life as it comes and refrain from subjecting yourself to the anxiousness and panic that too much worry can cause. Life is stressful enough, so don't make it harder than it has to be.

The third is a funny one but also holds true. "For a happy life, you need two things, a clean conscience and a clean colon. Because nothing kills you faster than carrying around crap you don't need." (Rev. Matthew Thomas.) This one means that we need to remember to release things that burden us, or we will be carrying unnecessary toxic weight around with us. I say it can kill you because a clogged colon obviously is a health problem, and emotionally, a clogged conscience creates stress on your nervous system. Walk softly. Speak kindly. Be gentle with yourself.

The fourth and last saying is, "It matters not what the world is doing, but what you are doing in the world." (Rev. Matthew Thomas.) Akin to the first one by Douglas Monroe, this saying also reminds us to concern ourselves with our own purpose and journey. Though we interact within this world with everyone else, we don't want to make someone else's problems our problems too.

In conclusion, I wish everyone a safe, joyous, and bountiful journey. May our creator bless your every step, and if I'm lucky, our journeys might intersect someday.

Rev. Matthew Thomas is a husband and father, US Army Veteran, Universal Life Church ordained minister, hedge druid, reiki master teacher, master seer, clairvoyant / psychic artist, and of course, an empath. When this book was published, he resided in Fleetwood, Berks County, PA. He serves the greater pagan community at large, providing instruction, personal spiritual counseling, rites of passage, and healing services.

Rev. Thomas works as a healer of many facets: a reiki master teacher and researcher of holistic energy healing, and he began serving as a CNA in a hospital emergency room through the 2020 Covid-19 pandemic. Focusing his abilities as an empath, Rev. Thomas plans to eventually become an end-of-life chaplain in hospice care and author books on the subject of practical spiritual growth in the 21st century and the physics of energy therapies and their practical value in modern medicine. Keep your eyes open for his first book entitled "Witch one am I."

The Power of the Empath
By YuSon Shin

Healer, Teacher, Author, and Speaker

A common perception of an empath is that the person is "too emotional," "too sensitive," and "weak." Instead, I propose that empaths possess superpowers, most notably, the power to heal. Often the word "sensitive" is used to describe empaths, sometimes resulting in a knee-jerk negative connotation. However, empaths bring a lot of heart into everything they do and are essentially a big bunch of feelers and healers.

Empaths have a higher level of sensitivity that enables them to put themselves in someone else's shoes, giving them an elevated vantage point of another person's perspective that not everyone has. Although there are some drawbacks to being an empath, the benefits reveal themselves once the empath becomes a master of their personal energy as well as the energy of those around them.

The ability to feel what others are going through at a deep empathic level allows them to better understand the emotions, pain, and struggles of others. This ability even applies to people who hold opposing beliefs which can help the empath spread understanding that supports tolerance and acceptance of differences which we so desperately need more of in this world.

Studies even show that highly empathic people may be able to feel another person's physical pain. This ability guides empaths to be peacemakers, connectors, fantastic friends, great listeners, and healers. Having insight into the emotions of people who might be putting on the mask of a brave face allows empaths to make inroads in helping people to open up, give good advice, build relationships, and form strong social bonds with others. Empaths even have the power to interpret nuances of feelings. Ultimately, we all want to feel understood, and empaths can do that more frequently and at a deeper level than most.

In my life, I feel fortunate that I am able to see and feel the power of being an empath. While I understand the benefits of being an empath now, I was taught growing up to stuff my feelings inside and deny anything non-logical due to my Korean-American upbringing. Although difficult, especially as an empath, having a hot-tempered and abusive father required me to develop the ability to read the room quickly. It gave me more opportunities to use and grow my beautiful gift of being able to feel into people.

Even though I have overcome the struggles of my youth, I can still get triggered and revert to my old ways. These lessons have been invaluable, but a guide's explanation, as a child or an adult, would have been so helpful.

Much like a superhero with newfound superpowers, I struggled with being an empath until I understood, acknowledged, and flexed my empathic muscles by practicing my ability to feel. I had to embrace my gifts and make them a part of me. However, the early days were not without mishaps. I made every mistake imaginable, and like the exaggerations of the cartoons, I went through an awkward stage where I pursued my gifts as if it were something outside of myself to reign in and capture.

Often, I misjudged my powers or had my powers backfire and implode on me, much like the Wile E. Coyote in pursuit of the Road Runner. These events would happen most often when I did one of these two things.

First, when I would stuff my feelings inside for so long that they would inevitably either explode or implode.

Second, when I would read someone's emotional state and forget that emotions are fluid and not fixed. This means that my decisions would be based on my perception of a fixed emotional state without reevaluating the current conditions and considering how they might change or affect the situation. Insert image of Wile E. Coyote continuing to run after he travels off the edge of a cliff only to find that when his momentum ends, he falls into a deep canyon, causing a puff of dust to rise down below.

In this case, life takes on the role of the Road Runner, giving me a knowing look and a "beep beep," not in a judgmental or vengeful way, but as a simple signal of acknowledgment. In reality, all I had to do was look and develop the power within.

Unlike my whirlwind pursuit of the strengths of empathy outside of myself, my internal feeling tank was always calm, strong, full, and aligned with source. It was always there, patiently waiting for me to tap in.

The hardest but most important lesson I learned was to have strong boundaries. Like most empaths, I am a giver by nature and prone to attracting narcissists and energy vampires. I have collected more than a few of these in my life, especially in the romantic relationship department, and these people tend to stick around like flies to flypaper.

They need attention and energy, and a great majority have developed charisma and magnetism to help them get what they want. Initially, it feels so nice, and even intoxicating, to have their attention focused on you. Whether it be boyfriends or friends, I would give until it hurt me. I would voluntarily take their energetic baggage until I was weighed down to the point of immobility. It seemed like the polite thing to do at the time.

The kicker is they would feel freer and more energetic than ever to pursue their interests and dreams while I was too exhausted from giving all my energy and taking their energetic baggage to even think about mine. They needed healing, and, as healers, we are there and eager to help, and that is how empaths and narcissists often find each other.

Without strong boundaries, what should be a healer-healee relationship can often cross over into a romantic parasitic relationship, and then we so often slap a label on it, calling it "love." It never occurred to me, until wisdom set in with age, that I could simply refuse the energy or put it down permanently if it were thrust upon me. I also taught myself to clean house energetically and rid myself of these soul-sucking energy vampires. Spring cleaning is not just for spring and not just for the home. The nagging feeling of being victimized disappeared when I set strong boundaries for myself.

People are attracted to the warmth and compassion of empaths. Empaths are fantastic listeners, and people are drawn in by this gift. I often experience this firsthand when strangers talk to me about their most personal problems, often revealing closely held secrets. I have had many hours usurped by people who wanted to pour their hearts out because they needed an outlet, and I felt safe to them. I didn't have the heart to interrupt them just to rush to my next engagement. The importance of the gym seems insignificant next to issues of abuse or struggles with sexual identity or depression.

While this immediate trust is flattering and having a strong connection with another person feels so good, empaths can become a dumping ground for other people's problems. Those lines between a good person and a dumping ground quickly blur without clear boundaries set in place.

Even though I am an empathic feeler, I am also a dominantly left-brained, logic-based analyzer, so it pleased me to find there is science backing empathy. A leading neuroscientist named Marco Iacoboni explains mirror neurons and their connection to empathy in his book *Mirroring People: The Science of Empathy and How We Connect with Others.* These mirror neurons in the brain may help us mirror the emotions of others. They are a type of brain cell that responds equally when we perform an action and when that action is performed by someone else and merely witnessed.

For example, when you see someone get slapped across the face, you recoil in sympathy and can almost feel the sting of the aggression. Or you watch an Olympic swimmer compete, and you find your heart racing, and you're mimicking the arm movements of their swim strokes. It seems, as mirror neurons are strongly linked to empathy, some people may have more mirror neurons than others. Empathy has varying levels or degrees like on a spectrum. Iacoboni explains in his "broken mirror hypothesis" that autism may be a result of malfunctioning mirror neurons.

The most optimistic and beneficial trait of empathy, like intuition, is its ability to be heightened and developed with practice. Like working out, getting better and more accurate feelers requires regular exercise. With much practice, you can develop into an empath with six-pack feelers. I call them my "Spidey senses." Empathy can provide the emotional intelligence facet to logic or knowledge-based intelligence. Boom! When these two aspects come together, you create a magical and well-rounded person.

My empathic abilities have also been a key component of my healing work. I knew I was a healer before I knew I was an empath, intuitive, medium, or medical medium. As a young person, my hand would instinctively know to go to the location of someone's pain. My hand would get hot, and after a few minutes, they would feel better. My mom would ask me as a child to give her back massages.

People would also feel better after just speaking to me and telling me their secrets. Animals would gravitate towards me. These are all tell-tale signs of a healer, and I recognized that I had this ability. But the abilities of an empath, intuitive, medium, or medical medium were for "special" people, and I couldn't wrap my brain around it to "own it" and believe I was also one of those "special" people until much later in life. The ability to feel another person's pain, emotions, energy, and even intentions have far-reaching healing benefits.

Empaths see the world uniquely because they feel into things rather than solely relying on their eyes.

Spidey senses may even help save a life. About four years ago, I took part in an all-day group activity involving a series of obstacle courses like climbing a rock wall, climbing a very tall pole and jumping to grab a donut shape, walking a tight rope, etc.

I finished climbing the pole, and as I readied myself to make the dizzying leap to the donut, I saw everyone running across the field, including those who were supposed to hold the rope attached to my harness. I managed to get down and investigate the flurry of activity. As a short person, I could see nothing behind a mass of standing bodies. Someone of authority knew I was a healer and grabbed me by the shoulders and set me in front of the man on the ground who had lost consciousness.

One person was giving CPR chest compressions, another was giving breaths, and another held his hand and was actively giving reiki energy. My empathic powers allowed me to feel into his body. I immediately knew that he had had a heart attack, and he was out of his body completely. I sent remote energy healing directly to his heart and telepathically, repeatedly, asked his spirit to come back to his body.

It took a long handful of minutes, but then I saw his soul re-enter his body. I read about a silver cord that attaches the soul to the body, and although I don't usually see things with my physical eyes, I saw the split-second re-entry. The unconscious man took a deep breath and was ready for a fight as he immediately pushed people off.

After he was transported to a hospital by the paramedics, the remaining group huddled together, formed a circle while holding hands, and said a prayer. We were told that he didn't have a heart condition, but I knew better. I felt that he had had a heart attack, and he would require surgery for multiple bypasses. This ability to feel allowed me to direct the healing energy to where his heart needed it most. Bringing this man back was a group effort. I am happy to report that the gentleman is doing well today.

I hope no one has to experience a crisis of health like this, especially with a loved one, but the ability to feel helped in this situation immensely.

Long-distance empathy can also be used to feel into someone yards or thousands of miles away with the same level of accuracy. Covid forced me to transition my healing practice to remote only. Whether the session is on the phone or via Zoom, I can scan anyone's body for their current physical condition and send healing energy directly to the source of the pain or illness.

In mediumship, this empathic ability can be used to give evidence as to how a person in spirit died or their physical state before their passing. This magical ability to feel can also tap into their personality, emotional state, struggles, and even their relationship to the client.

Now that I have embraced and am in control of my empathic superpowers, I am driven to teach this skill to others so they can utilize their feelers to propel their lives forward and learn how to make their lives flow more easily. Empaths see the world uniquely because they feel into things rather than solely relying on their eyes. We are likely to pick up on things other people miss or make connections that are not clear to others.

Additionally, empaths can make excellent human lie detectors. I want all empaths to be able to efficiently identify and cut out energy vampires, narcissists, liars, and emotionally stunted people. For example, I no longer allow people to take my energy now that I have learned to maintain healthy boundaries.

I am now able to differentiate the feelings and emotions of others from my own, and I have learned to cope with and prevent sensory and emotional overload. I honor my energy, my need to recharge, and my energy exchanges with others, and I do not feel the impulse to have exchanges out of politeness if they don't feel right. I have learned to control my energetic field, and I have become my own source of energy.

Empaths have superpowers, and we should embrace them. Barack Obama spoke about the "empathy deficit" in America. He also said "…Empathy is a quality of character that can change the world." Empaths are superheroes that are greatly needed. Grab your cape!

YuSon Shin is a healer, intuitive, medium, medical medium, speaker, author, and teacher of the healing and intuitive arts. She helps individuals heal themselves using past life, karma, and ancestral clearing techniques utilizing the Akashic records and Chinese energy healing. She is also a practitioner of the bengston energy healing method, reiki (usui, archangel & kundalini), integrated energy therapy, 5th dimensional quantum healing, quantum touch, DNA theta, and access bars. Her passion is teaching and helping people awaken their spiritual gifts and superpowers. She is an author and speaker. You can reach her at www.ShinHealingArts.com.

I Couldn't Wine it Away:
A Recovery Story
By Meg Lewis, CPRC, SRCD

Recovery and Life Coach

It had been three months since I stopped drinking. I referred to it as "retiring my corkscrew." I'm not so sure I was missing my wine as much as I was missing the relief wine gave me.

I never considered myself a woman with a drinking problem, but stopping was a soul calling, one I resisted for many years. There was a persistent nudge, and the more I was nudged, the more I would drink. I just wanted it to stop talking to me, to leave me alone. Life was challenging enough, and drinking made socializing and dealing with all the stress so much easier.

When I didn't answer the nudge, I was given a great big push: An accident in my home, painful enough to get my attention, but thankfully not enough to leave any permanent physical scars.

There I sat in front of my computer, feeling all the feelings and not really being able to identify who I was. There was a feeling of desperation. In the search bar, I typed "Help." No, that wouldn't do. I backspaced, and typed "Who am I?" No, that wasn't it either. I thought for a few more minutes and typed "Sober identity." That was it: "Who am I now that I am sober?" That was where my journey to wholeness began.

That fortuitous search led me to my recovery coach and the one I will always refer to as my angel. As she had written a book and started a business with the same name, *"Sober Identity,"* I believe it was a divine match. Her gentleness, experience, and teachings steeped with spiritual principles strengthened my resolve and self-worth.

Shortly after I started working with her, I kept seeing articles on social media. Titles like "Are you an empath?" repeatedly appeared on my feed. So much so that I had no choice but to finally read one. My initial thought was, "Whoa, is that it? Is that what I am? "

Now that I was not drinking, was that why my feelings were so intense, why colors were now appearing so vibrant, sounds were so loud, and life seemed so much clearer? Was that why I couldn't handle being in crowds of people, and sometimes I just "knew things" without ever having an explanation of how?

Suddenly, so much of my life made sense, but this explanation felt so "out there." Although I had been embracing my spiritual side, this seemed too "woo woo" even for me. At the end of one of our sessions, I took a deep breath and asked my recovery coach, "Have you ever heard of an empath? Do you think I am an empath?"

Now I cringe, thinking those are such crazy questions. Yet her response surprised me because she said, "Of course you are, and I am sorry we haven't talked about this yet. Most people with addictions are empaths." She said it so matter of factly. All that came to mind was Glinda the Good Witch saying, "You've had the power all along." I paused and asked, "Is this a good thing or a bad thing? Is this a blessing or a curse? What do I do with it?" I can't remember her exact response, but it was along the line of "Do you have to do anything with it?" I thought for a long while and decided to tuck it away for the moment. I had so much more to focus on.

The first memory I have of an empathic experience occurred when I was seven years old. I had a best friend who lived down the street. One Friday night, I begged to sleep over at her house, but my mother inexplicably refused to let me go. Later that night, my friend and her two brothers perished in a house fire. Their mother frantically tried to reach them, but she was forced to jump out of a second-story window, leaving her children behind and her paralyzed.

Of course, this trauma was a lot for a seven-year-old to process. I did miss my friend, but it was the "feelings" that were much more overwhelming. I remember feeling so strongly about what they experienced that night, almost as if I was there with them. I can see their mother searching for them, calling for them, and her anguish at having to jump. I felt her pain for so long. The feelings were far beyond the comprehension of a child that young.

At some point after their deaths, my friend's mother had her daughter's bicycle delivered to me. It was a loving gesture on her part, something that made her feel connected. I didn't know why at the time, but I could never touch that bike, for it was saturated with smothering grief.

The following year, I was bullied in school, and my teacher, who was well past her prime, called me "stupid" in front of my class. Those experiences carved thoughts of unworthiness and incompetence in my tender soul. Combined with the anxiety and grief from the year before, I was unable to develop and express my true identity.

I became a people pleaser and began to act the way I thought people wanted me to. Since I believed the real me was unlikable, I needed to figure out how to be liked. I went along with everyone else, often ignoring my own intuition and needs. Because I also believed I was stupid, I struggled throughout school, and "I can't" became my mantra.

Despite the early traumas and my negative beliefs, I had a good life: a loving husband, family, home, career, and good friends. I battled myself when I tried making new friends, but what ended up being my greatest struggle was taking on emotions that did not belong to me. I did not realize it was happening, nor did I realize the impact it was having.

I was the one everyone looked at during the sad part of a movie- they would ask, "Is she crying yet?" Of course, I was crying and was probably crying just anticipating the sad part. Eventually, I became more discerning of what movies I could tolerate watching, although it felt like something about me was broken.

Many years ago, I read the book, *The Bridges of Madison County,* by Robert James Waller. The author so articulately described the pain of lost love that I was overcome with grief for a month as if I was experiencing this loss myself. I had trouble eating and concentrating and could not even begin to explain why I was experiencing this grief in my body. As with the movies, I had to become more discerning about what I could read, again making me feel like this was something that was "wrong" with me.

My chosen career in healthcare has also greatly impacted me, for the grief of all those who have lost a loved one is permanently etched on my soul. I can remember where I was, who was there, and the reactions of those who witnessed or learned of the passing of their loved ones. The tears, the screams, and the cries had to be compartmentalized and tucked deeply away.

Grief wasn't the only emotion that clung to me. There was anxiety, frustration, and anger. If there was chaos going on around me, I felt as if it was mine. I didn't know where it ended, and I began. The strain of the emotional overload had taken its toll. There were times of feeling great darkness and several attempts with mood-altering medications. The medications helped with the heaviness, but the other side effects became intolerable, and I had to stop them. Although I had always enjoyed a few glasses of wine here and there, a few glasses of wine became the medicine that helped me hold it together, at least at first.

As my children got a little older and required less hands-on care, it became more convenient for me to have a few glasses of wine to unwind from the day. It also made the weekend socializing much more fun. I was more at ease, and I forgot how awkward I was in social settings. My more relaxed disposition made it easier "to be me." I was funny, and everyone else was funny too. Of course, as many of the stories go, a few glasses of wine became my warm-up. The first two were my medicine, and the rest were for fun.

As time went on, my drinking increased. My sons grew older, and life seemed fun despite the more frequent lost days to hangovers. At some point, I developed an internal nudging to stop drinking. I argued with it, and I rationalized it. I did not drink every day and often volunteered as a designated driver. Clearly no problem here. There were a few events I hosted where I couldn't drink until they were over. It wasn't until it was time to clean up that I started getting edgy because I wanted it to be over so I could get to the after-party. That was my time to relax and drink. A few people commented that they didn't like the Meg who didn't drink because "She's no fun." These events reinforced my belief that I was still in control and if I did not drink, I was still unlikable.

The nudging persisted, and so did the rationalizing. It seemed like my drinking was the same as my peers', but many things kept nudging me and created so much shame: forgotten commitments and conversations, falling asleep at the table, or failing to take out the dog.

As my shame increased, so did my anxiety. Drinking had become a reason for celebration, a way to connect with others, and a solution for life's stress. I could not see how I could function without it, despite the things bringing so much shame to my life.

When I continued to ignore the nudging, the Universe gave me a great big shove. I had burned my leg from thigh to foot. In the days that followed, I had no choice but to surrender.

My internal guidance, higher self or whatever you would like to call it, had my undivided attention. She spoke lovingly yet firmly. She told me that if I did not stop drinking, I would die. I had much more to achieve in my life, and it would be impossible if I continued this path. Oddly, I had heard this voice before. This voice had saved my life on several occasions, and I knew I had to heed this warning.

I came to understand that worthiness, belonging, and joy were my birthright, and if lovingly protecting myself caused others to feel slighted, it was not my responsibility.

Choosing to recover from alcohol allowed me to restore the life that I never truly developed. Discovering I was an empath and what that meant was a turning point in my journey. Understanding that being an empath was at the opposite end of being a narcissist; they feel too little, and we feel too much. Although being an empath is not considered a mental health disorder as narcissism is, it is often diagnosed as an anxiety disorder, according to Dr. Judith Orloff, author of *The Empath's Survival Guide: Life Strategies for Sensitive People.*

Once I was able to clear my head from the fog of alcohol and with my new understanding of myself, I set forth on my journey, practicing recovery and spiritual principles. I learned to honor myself by feeling all my feelings, and with great intention, I was able to discern my feelings from others.' I was now able to bear witness to and hold space for others' grief. I no longer thought I was weird because I had to protect my heart from movies, books, and, sadly, daily news. I came to understand that if I allowed it, everything could break my heart. What I gave my attention to mattered as much as with whom I spent my time.

I came to understand that worthiness, belonging, and joy were my birthright, and if lovingly protecting myself caused others to feel slighted, it was not my responsibility. I sometimes still struggle with saying "no," but it's part of the radical self-care required for a healthy me. I've come to understand that the parts of me that I thought made me weird, like anxiety in crowds, hating loud music, not having quiet and alone time, and feeling over-stimulated with too many things to do, were not weird. It's just me.

There are positive attributes of being an empath that I did not wholly recognize. I have a deep connection to my intuition. I must be intentional, and when I am, I receive guidance that is never wrong. This guidance saved my life on many occasions and is responsible for the amazing existence that sobriety has given me.

I have a "knowing." This knowing could be part of my intuition, but it feels different to me. When I get hit with a "knowing," without a doubt, it will be. It is difficult to explain, but it is not just wishful thinking or having faith.

I can read energy. No, I cannot read your mind, but I am likely to be able to "feel" how you are feeling. Not only does it give me the ability to know what to say or not say, but it also allows me to connect on a deeper level. Conversely, I can also tell when someone is being inauthentic.

I have a connection with spirit. This is an attribute I have not cultivated. My first spirit encounter was after my friend died in the fire at the age of seven. I was not afraid of her visit, yet I did not like it either. I once jokingly asked a recently deceased family member which tool I needed for the task. I went to the workroom, and immediately the wrench I needed jumped off the hook onto the workbench in front of me. I ran out of there so fast, shouting "thank you" over my shoulder. I also randomly receive messages for others from their loved ones. Occasionally I have passed them along, but sometimes I don't feel like I understand this connection well enough to put myself in that situation.

Kindness, compassion, and empathy, all on a healthy level, are my superpowers. One of my favorite quotes from Philip James Bailey is "Kindness is Wisdom." That quote hung at my desk for years. I would never wish being bullied on anyone, but it was the catalyst for me to embody those characteristics.

I never wanted anyone to experience the pain I had felt from my actions or the words I had spoken. Not only did I not want to cause harm, but I also wished to make everyone feel included, heard, seen, and understood. It took many years to balance this because it was easy to neglect myself while wholly embracing others.

In hindsight, I realize that when I typed "sober identity" into the search bar, I was really looking for my true self. I've learned so much and have come full circle now. I have embraced the gifts of being an empath and learned to navigate the hard parts.

Life is clearer and louder and far more beautiful than I can describe.

If you are an empath, you may be wondering what you can do with it? Is it a good or bad thing? Is this a blessing or a curse? The answer is yes, it can be all of those things.

It's what we are willing to embrace and learn that will decide which way it goes. At times it can feel like all those things at once, but in the end, it's just who we are. Love and protect yourself fiercely.

Meg Lewis is an empath in long-term recovery who went on to train and become certified as a recovery coach, life coach, and a SHE RECOVERS coach designate. She's a proud wife, mother, and grandmother, dedicated to living her life as a positive role model. Meg coaches clients privately and is a volunteer at SHE RECOVERS and within her local community. You can learn more about Meg at www.MegLewisCoaching.com.

THE EMPATH EFFECT

Thank you so much!

T hank you greatly for reading and enjoying this book full of authentic stories from the heart. Every author in here shared a piece of their true selves with you, and that is a beautiful experience.

This book is an unexpected tool for healing. The first time I read it, it softened me, opened me, and helped me process emotional baggage.

These are real people sharing their real lives and how they overcame their life circumstances. We are not the circumstance that we are in. We are love. We are meant to give and receive love, and if that means altering your life situation completely, then so be it. This book healed pieces of my heart and soul. I sincerely hope it helped you too.

I would like to invite you to give us a star rating and leave an honest review on whichever platform you found the book. Which story was your favorite? Which author did you connect with the most?

Every empath has an effect. What's yours?

Feel free to connect with me!

Find me online at HealingLightEmpath.com

Join our amazing Facebook group for Beginner Empaths at Facebook.com/Groups/BeginnerEmpath

Sign up for our mailing list so you can hear about all the fun new activities before they happen!

https://HealingLightEmpath.com/signup

With sincere love and gratitude,

Alicia McBride

Made in the USA
Las Vegas, NV
17 March 2022

45842814R00144